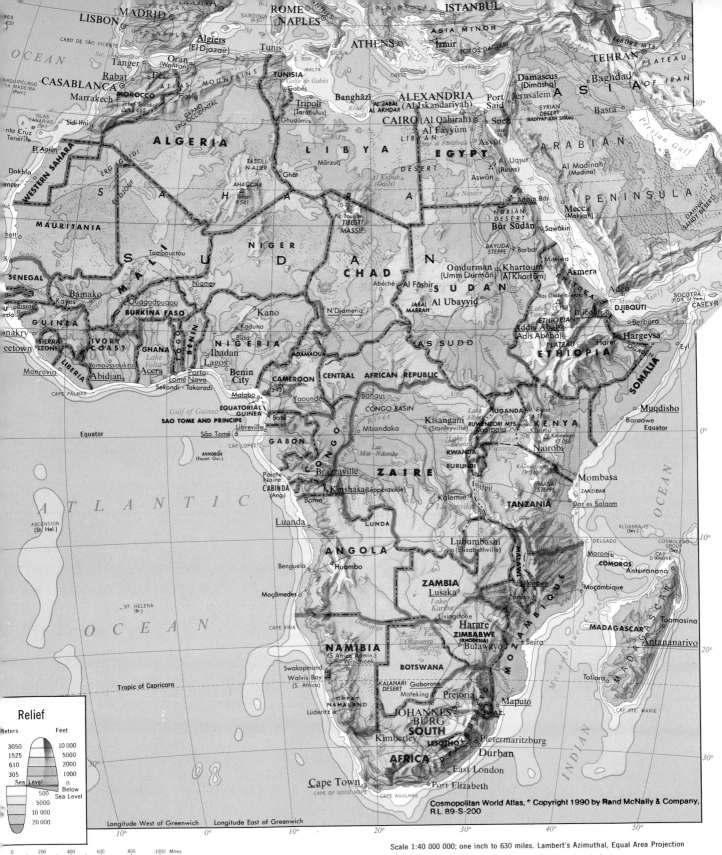

LISBON MADRID ROME ISTANBUL

CABO DE SÃO VICENTE SARDINIA NAPLES ASIA MINOR

OCEAN Algiers (El Djazair) Tunis ATHENS Izmir TOROS DAĞLARI ELBURZ MTS.

CASABLANCA Tanger Oran (Wahran) TUNISIA MALTA CYPRUS Damascus (Dimashq) TEHRĀN PLATEAU Baghdād

Marrakech Fès Figuig ATLAS MOUNTAINS Tripoli (Tarābulus) Banghāzī ALEXANDRIA (Al Iskandariyah) Port Said Jerusalem ASIA Basra GULF OF IRAN

MOROCCO Jebel Toubkal 4,165 Gabès Golfe de Gabès AL JABAL AL AKHDAR SYRIAN DESERT (BĀDIYAT ASH SHĀM)

Sidi Ifni ERG OCCIDENTAL Ghudāmis CAIRO (Al Qāhirah) Al Fayyūm Suez

ISLAS CANARIAS (Sp.) ALGERIA LIBYA EGYPT ARABIAN Mecca (Makkah) DAHNA (SANDY DESERT)

El Aaiún Marzūq LIBYAN DESERT Asyūṭ Aswān Al Uqsur (Luxor) Al Madinah (Medina)

WESTERN SAHARA Ghāt TASSILI-N-AJJER AHAGGAR Tahat 9,541 Pic Toussidé TIBESTI MASSIF Lake Nasser NUBIAN DESERT PENINSULA

MAURITANIA SAHARA NIGER CHAD Admin. Bdy. Būr Sūdān Sawākin Barbar BAYUDA STEPPE Mitsiwa Asmera ERITREA Aden GULF OF ADEN SOCOTRA (P.D.R. of Yemen) CAP CASEYR

SENEGAL Tombouctou Niamey Kano N'Djamena SUDAN Al Fāshir JABAL MARRAH Al Ubayyiḍ Omdurman (Umm Durmān) Khartoum (Al Kharṭūm) Ras Dashen Terara 15,158 ETHIOPIAN Addis Ababa (Adīs Abeba) DJIBOUTI Djibouti Hargeysa

Bamako Kayes MALI BURKINA FASO Ouagadougou Kaduna Bida NIGERIA ADAMAOUA AS SUDD PLATEAU Harer OGADEN Eyl

GUINEA Bissau SIERRA LEONE IVORY COAST GHANA BENIN Ibadan Lagos Benin City CAMEROON CENTRAL AFRICAN REPUBLIC Uele Lake Turkana ETHIOPIA SOMALIA

Freetown LIBERIA Yamoussoukro Abidjan Accra Lomé Porto Novo Sekondi-Takoradi Malabo Yaoundé Bangui Uele Lake Albert RUWENZORI MTS. Kampala UGANDA Mt. Elgon 14,178 KENYA Muqdisho

Monrovia CAPE PALMAS Gulf of Guinea EQUATORIAL GUINEA SÃO TOMÉ AND PRINCIPE Bata GABON Libreville CONGO Mbandaka CONGO BASIN Kisangani (Stanleyville) Lake Victoria Kisumu Kitinyaga (Kenya) 17,058 Nairobi Baraawe Equator

Equator SÃO TOMÉ CAP LOPEZ ANNOBÓN (Equat. Gui.) Lac Mai-Ndombe River RWANDA BURUNDI Lake Kivu MASAI STEPPE Kilimanjaro 19,340 Mombasa

Pointe Noire Brazzaville Kinshasa (Léopoldville) ZAIRE Uvira Lake Tanganyika ZANZIBAR Dar es Salaam

CABINDA (Ang.) Boma Kalemie TANZANIA

ATLANTIC Luanda LUNDA ASCENSION (St. Hel.) CAP DELGADO ALDABRA IS. (Sey.)

OCEAN Benguela Huambo ANGOLA Lubumbashi (Elisabethville) MALAWI COSMOLEDO GROUP (Fr.) Moroni COMOROS Antsiranana CAP D'AMBRE

ST. HELENA (Br.) ZAMBIA Lusaka Lake Kariba Livingstone Blantyre MOZAMBIQUE Moçambique MADAGASCAR

Moçamedes Victoria Falls Harare Zambezi Beira Toamasina

CAPE FRIA Okavango ZIMBABWE (RHODESIA) Bulawayo Antananarivo

Tropic of Capricorn NAMIBIA (S. Africa Admin.) Okavango Swamp BOTSWANA KALAHARI DESERT Gaborone Pretoria Maputo Toliara CAP STE. MARIE

Swakopmund Windhoek SWAZ. INDIAN

Walvis Bay (S. Africa) Mafeking JOHANNESBURG SOUTH LESOTHO Pietermaritzburg OCEAN

Lüderitz GREAT NAMALAND Gaborone Kimberley AFRICA Durban

Cape Town CAPE OF GOOD HOPE CAPE AGULHAS East London Port Elizabeth

Relief

Meters		Feet
3050		10 000
1525		5000
610		2000
305		1000
Sea Level		0
		Below Sea Level
500		
5000		
10 000		
20 000		

Longitude West of Greenwich Longitude East of Greenwich

Scale 1:40 000 000; one inch to 630 miles. Lambert's Azimuthal, Equal Area Projection

Elevations and depressions are given in feet.

0 200 400 600 800 1000 Miles

0 400 800 1200 1600 Kilometers

Enchantment of the World

ALGERIA

By Marlene Targ Brill

Consultant for Algeria: Robert Mortimer, Ph.D., Department of Political Science, Haverford College, Haverford, Pennsylvania

Consultant for Reading: Robert L. Hillerich, Ph.D., Bowling Green State University, Bowling Green, Ohio

 CHILDRENS PRESS ®

CHICAGO

A nomad feeding his camel in the desert

Picture Acknowledgments
AP/Wide World Photos, Inc.: 38 (2 photos), 40 (2 photos), 42 (2 photos), 43, 45, 49, 50, 51, 53, 56 (left), 74 (left)
© **Victor Englebert:** Cover, 9 (right), 10 (left), 12, 13 (left), 14, 17 (right), 61, 80 (top left), 84 (left), 90 (left), 91 (left), 92, 95 (right), 96 (right), 98 (right), 111 (left)
© **Virginia Grimes:** 82
H. Armstrong Roberts: 91 (right); © **M. Koene**, 97, 116; © **G. Tortoli**, 17 (left), 67
Historical Pictures Service, Chicago: 18 (right), 20 (left), 22, 23, 27, 30 (2 photos), 31 (right), 32 (right), 33, 70, 71, 75
Journalism Services: © **Duffour**, 80 (bottom left); © **Rongier**, 90 (right)
North Wind Picture Archives: 18 (left), 21 (2 photos), 25, 31 (left), 32 (left)
© **Photri:** 6 (top right), 10 (right), 16 (2 photos), 20 (right), 56 (right), 74 (right), 77 (right), 80 (top right), 84 (right), 88 (right), 104 (4 photos), 109, 110 (2 photos), 113 (top & bottom left); © **M. Fantin**, 111 (right)
Root Resources: © **John Chitty**, 6 (top left), 9 (left), 63 (right), 90 (center), 98 (left), 99, 113 (right); © **Kenneth W. Fink**, 13 (right)
Shostal Associates: 4, 5, 6 (bottom), 11, 54, 58 (bottom), 64, 65, 66 (left), 77 (left), 83 (right), 85 (left), 87, 93 (right), 94, 95 (left), 96 (left), 100 (bottom), 102 (right), 103, 105, 106, 107, 108 (right); © **H. Kanus**, 58 (top), 85 (right), 93 (left), 100 (top), 108 (left), 112
Superstock International Ltd.: 11, 102 (left)
Valan: © **Kennon Cooke**, 63 (left); © **Val & Alan Wilkinson**, 60, 66 (right), 72, 80 (bottom right), 83 (left & center), 88 (left)
Len W. Meents: Maps on 104, 107, 110
Courtesy Flag Research Center, Winchester, Massachusetts 01890: Flag on back cover
Cover: A view of Ghardaia

Library of Congress Cataloging-in-Publication Data

Targ Brill, Marlene.
    Algeria / by Marlene Targ Brill.
       p.   cm. — (Enchantment of the world)
    Summary: Discusses the geography, history, people, and culture of this large country in northern Africa.
    ISBN 0-516-02717-4
    1. Algeria—Juvenile literature.   [1.   Algeria.]
I.   Title.   II.   Series.
DT275.T37   1990
965—dc20   89-25436
                                                   CIP
                                                    AC

Cultivated lands in the mountains

TABLE OF CONTENTS

Mountain villages (above) in the Grand Kabylie, the old narrow streets of the city of Ghardaia (right), and a very contemporary scene in Algiers

Chapter 1

A LAND OF CONTRASTS

Picture snow-covered mountains overlooking dusty desert or black-pebbled plateaus blending into a sea of red sand. Hear loudspeakers blaring the call to Friday afternoon prayer being drowned out by car horns in overcrowded city streets; streets filled with people in veils and Western dress. These are the sights and sounds of Algeria. To an outsider they contradict each other. They clash. Algeria is a land of contrasts.

Few countries can claim such diversity. Yet, few countries struggle so hard to establish a single identity. Algeria is an evolving nation—thrust into a modern world in 1962 after 132 years of French domination. Perhaps more than any country in Africa, Algeria is marked by colonial conquest and the size of European population that migrated to its shores. Only a varied geography protected some Algerians from complete defeat, while exposing others to massive changes from foreign oppression.

PEOPLE OF THE MAGHRIB

Algeria, the second-largest nation in Africa, extends 750 miles (1,200 kilometers) along the Mediterranean Sea on the northwest coast of Africa. It is part of a region that early Arab conquerors called *jazirat al maghrib*, "the island of the west." The island refers to the block of land that lies between the Mediterranean Sea to the north and the Sahara desert on the south, separating it from the rest of Africa. Today, that land includes Morocco to Algeria's west and Tunisia and part of Libya to the east. Algeria also borders Mauritania, Mali, and Niger to the south.

Most people of the Maghrib share a common history that brings similarities in language, religion, and culture. However, independent Algerian groups never organized around a central government before colonization, as in neighboring countries. Perhaps this disunity encouraged France, Algeria's colonial ruler, to try and destroy any sense of tradition the Algerians had.

DIVERSE LAND

Algeria's land contributes to the isolation and diversity of people to this day. The country ranges from damp, overpopulated coastal regions to empty, dry deserts, with mountains, valleys, and plateaus in between. One of the greatest inconsistencies of Algeria is its size. Algeria is one-quarter the size of the United States or almost twice the size of the South American nation of Peru. Yet, only about 3 percent of the country is cultivated and 13 percent suitable for pasture. Most Algerians live along the fertile coastal region to the north. Independent groups nestle in rugged mountain villages near pastures and create colorful oasis communities in desert sands.

The easiest way to describe Algeria's geography is to divide the country into sections. Two east-west mountain ranges, the Tell Atlas comprising several connecting ranges to the north and the

Left: Flowers cover the northern fields during the rainy season.
Right: A public writer in the Aurès Mountains takes roadside dictation.

Saharan Atlas to the south, cut Algeria's 919,595 square miles
(2,381,741 square kilometers) into three main geographic regions.
Each has different landforms and offers varied opportunities to its
inhabitants.

TELL REGION

Most Algerian cities, and 90 percent of the population, occupy
the fertile coastal area called the *Tell*, which is Arabic for hill.
Here the effects of urban progress clash most vividly with
traditional values. However, the Tell originally earned its name
for the gently rolling hills and valleys that provide the country's
best farmland. Just west of the capital, Algiers, lie citrus groves
and vineyards cleared by the French from malaria-filled swamps.
Aleppo pine, juniper, and cork trees grow on the rugged
mountain slopes of the Kabylie and Aurès along the eastern coast
and southern part of the region.

El Kantara Gorge (left) and the rocky High Plateau region (right)

Most of the country's rivers are in the Tell, which keeps the land fertile. The rivers flood during the rainy season and drain into the Mediterranean. In summer they slow to a trickle or dry into sand.

Algerian weather varies according to geography. In the Tell the Mediterranean keeps the climate mild. Temperatures near the sea average a humid 77 degrees Fahrenheit (25 degrees Celsius) in summer and 52 degrees Fahrenheit (11 degrees Celsius) in the winter. Rainfall is scarce during stifling summers, but can bring 10 to 15 inches (25 to 38 centimeters) along the western coastline and up to 60 inches (152 centimeters) in the eastern Lesser Kabylie Mountains.

HIGH PLATEAU REGION

Southward is a High Plateau region soaring 1,300 to 4,300 feet (396 to 1,311 meters) above sea level between the Tell and Saharan mountains. Much of the flat plateau is rocky and dry. Cattle, sheep, and goats graze on small clumps, shrubs, scrub pine,

A shepherd and his flock

oak trees, and wild esparto grass dotting the plateau and grassland leading into the Saharan Atlas Mountains. Only about 7 percent of the people live here as herders. Some are nomads who go from pasture to pasture to feed their flocks from the grasses and shrubs that grow over most of the area.

Rainfall is limited. But during rainy seasons streams drain into shallow salt marshes, called *chotts*. Plateau temperatures are similar to those in the Tell, only slightly colder in winter.

What is unusual about plateau weather is the *sirocco*. This dusty, hot wind whips northward from the desert, blowing choking sand as far as the coastal Tell. Powerful sirocco winds sweep the High Plateaus from three to five weeks each summer.

Date palms, growing in a dry riverbed, surround Djanet oasis.

THE SAHARA

The folded rocks of the Saharan Atlas Mountains create the northernmost boundary of the Algerian Sahara desert. Once they were home to extensive Atlas cedar forests where wild sheep and a few desert gazelle roamed. But most trees were cut for fuel and building supplies. Now the mountains serve mainly as the gateway to the largest desert in the world.

The Algerian government has tried to curb the encroaching desert. The grandest project was the *barrage vert,* or green barrier. Rows of Aleppo pine trees have been planted along the Saharan Atlas ridge from Morocco to the Tunisian border. Unfortunately, the desert creeps northward quicker than workers can plant trees.

Hot, dry desert occupies more than 80 percent of the country. Still, Algeria's portion of the vast Sahara has more varied landscape than most people could imagine. Certainly there are large stretches of sand dunes within basins, or *ergs*, with shifting

The sand dunes of the Sahara (left); the desert fox, or fennec (right)

sands, stifling heat, and blinding sunlight. Underground rivers
offer the only water. The only life other than a few snakes, gerbils,
lizards, and the desert fox, or fennec, comes from isolated oasis
communities.

Oases look unusually built up for their location in the lifeless
desert. Deep green date palms, which sustain desert economy,
surround these communities. Three percent of the Algerians live
in the desert. Most settle on oases to grow dates and citrus fruits.
A few remain nomads, traveling between pastures with their
camels and other livestock. More recently, the northeast Sahara
sprouted derricks and rigs that pump the oil and natural gas that
lie beneath the desert.

To the south, the desert takes on many different looks. The
monotonous golden sea is transformed into plateaus of black
pebbles. Eventually, the plateaus melt into great spans of red sand.
Farther southeast, large sandstone rock formations signal the
beginning of the Ahaggar Mountains. Here Mount Tahat towers

The jagged peaks of the Ahaggar Mountains

9,573 feet (2,918 meters) over the desert, sometimes with snow on its peak. Many think it odd that this desert mountain is the highest peak in Algeria.

Few people come to this part of Algeria. A small part of the desert crosses the Tropic of Cancer, making temperatures painfully hot even in winter. Daytime temperatures have climbed to about 120 degrees Fahrenheit (49 degrees Celsius) in the midday sun. However, the dryness allows the air to cool quickly once the sun disappears. Evening temperatures can drop suddenly and seem freezing after the scorching daytime heat.

DIVERSE PEOPLE

Land provides the springboard for how Algerians live and work. But their customs and traditions are a blend of past influences and invading modern technology. Only by studying Algeria's origins will it become obvious how geography contributes to make Algeria a land of great contrast.

Chapter 2

LAND OF SURVIVORS

Algeria's history is a tale of survival. Centuries speak of the coming of a tribal people and their ability to last through seven major invasions. Through the years the people often changed religion, language, and work to satisfy their oppressors. Ruling culture built upon existing culture to alter the face of Algerian society. Yet, many characteristics of current Algeria originated long ago.

ANCIENT ALGERIA

Traces of prehistoric Algeria go back hundreds of thousands of years. The Bardo Museum in Algiers has a jawbone of a person who lived 500,000 years ago. But the most wonderful ancient finds are the colorful rock paintings discovered at Tassili-n-Ajjer in the South Sahara desert. About four thousand sandstone engravings— the largest collection of its kind—depict prehistoric African life spanning about 5,000 years.

North Africa was much different then. Land that is now the dusty, hot Sahara once blossomed with tropical grasses. Hippos lounged in the many lakes left after the Ice Age. Wandering hunters and herders roamed the countryside in search of buffalo

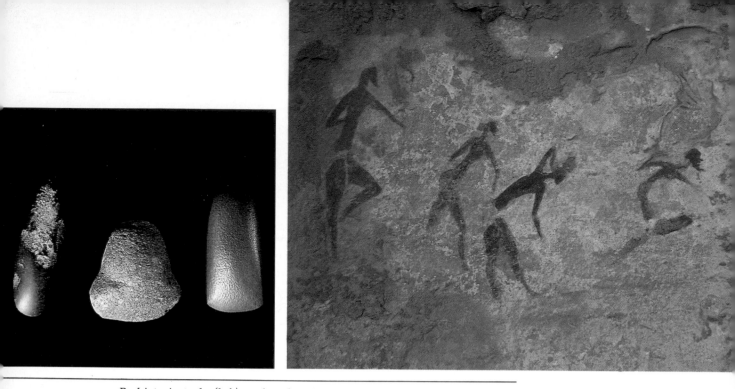

Prehistoric tools (left) and rock paintings at Tassili-n-Ajjer (right)

and food for their flocks. The earliest rock drawings about 6000 B.C. show crude figures in flared pants tied at the ankles shooting large buffalo with arrows. Somewhat later pictures indicate dark-skinned shepherds tending cattle in a country setting. In 1200 B.C., other stone artists added horse-drawn chariots like those from eastern Mediterranean cultures.

The pictorial diary ended around 1000 B.C. The climate became drier and the land harsher. Elephants, wild sheep, rhinoceroses, and giraffes left for damper regions. Most shepherds scattered south and east to avoid the advancing desert; others became part of the Berbers.

THE FREE MEN

The first people known in Algeria were the Berbers, who play an important role in the country today. Little is known of Berber origins. Some historians claim that Berbers migrated from

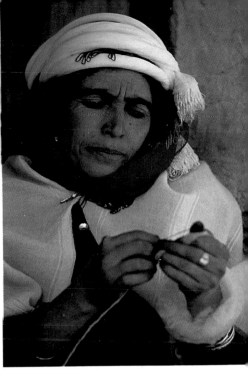

Mud huts in the Sahara (left);
a Berber woman spinning wool (right)

southwestern Asia in about 3000 B.C., following the
Mediterranean coast westward. Others pinpoint Berber beginnings
in Libya based on similarities between Berber language and
ancient Libyan writings. Researchers also associate ancient Berber
rug and pottery designs with those from southern Europe.

Despite strong links to other cultures, Berbers always
maintained an unmistakable identity. Their homes were either
tents or simple mud huts, depending upon whether they raised
horses and oxen or plowed land with sickles. Many Berbers
wandered throughout North Africa in hooded cloaks and tunics.
Berbers never had or wanted a nation of their own. Their loyalty
was to their family, clan, and tribe. They preferred to be called
imazighan, or free men.

Clans that came from the same Berber ancestors formed a group
headed by a chief. Land distribution was based solely upon who
worked the land. For centuries Berber groups fought to rule each
other and conquer their land. Nomads raided farmers continually.
However, the greatest threat to Berber culture came from foreign
invaders.

Phoenician sailors (above) arrived in galleys (right), seeking trading ports in the southern Mediterranean.

CARTHAGE AND ROME

Recorded history for Algeria and the entire Maghrib region began around the twelfth century B.C., after the arrival of Phoenician sailors. Phoenicians came from what is now Lebanon to scout trading ports along the southern Mediterranean. The most important Phoenician trading center developed outside Algeria in the city of Carthage (present-day Tunis). From here Phoenicians built their merchant empire.

Carthage enlisted Berber support by paying for trade rights. The two groups often sealed friendship treaties by a Berber chief marrying a woman from the Carthaginian royal family. Gradually, Phoenician trading posts sprang up along Algeria's coastline in Eikoci (Algiers), Rus (Skikda), and Hippo (Annaba). Phoenicians brought to the area their advanced farming techniques along with olive trees and the first grapevines for winemaking.

However, life changed little for Berbers, particularly nomads and inland farmers. Berbers accepted Carthage's authority, but looked to their own chieftains for leadership.

During the second century B.C., several Berber groups merged into larger kingdoms. Numidia, the northeastern and northcentral areas of Algeria today, became home to two kingdoms. A powerful king headed each kingdom. Farmers supported their king who, in turn, protected them from raiding nomads and invading powers.

The most noted Numidian king was Massinissa, who ruled around 200 B.C. Massinissa fought with Carthage in Spain. But when Rome defeated Carthage, he transferred his support to the Romans. With Roman backing, Massinissa united all of Numidia and established Cirta (now Constantine) as his seat of government. Massinissa's reign opened northern Algeria's door to Phoenician, Greek, and Roman advances in agriculture, economy, and culture. Although short-lived, Massinissa brought Numidia peace and prosperity.

Massinissa's son, Micipsa, kept his father's kingdom together until Romans destroyed Carthage in 146 B.C. Then Roman armies moved into Numidia to take greater control. Jugurtha, Massinissa's grandson, sought to reunite his grandfather's kingdom and led the Berbers in revolt against Rome. After a long and bitter war, a rival chieftain betrayed Jugurtha for part of Numidia as reward. Jugurtha died in a Roman jail. But Jugurtha and Massinissa's legacy as the first fighters for Algerian nationalism remains.

Rome needed North Africa to feed its vast empire and provide slaves. Berbers now rented their own land from Roman nobles and paid taxes to Rome with grain they grew. In return, Berbers in towns and the neighboring countryside gained a new common language, government, and identity. Today's ruins of cities, roads,

Left: Emperor Constantine   Right: Ruts from Roman chariot wheels can be seen in this ancient road in Timgad.

dams, and houses attest to improvements made under the Romans. However, mountain and desert groups kept their own identity through constant revolt.

Initially, religion was one area Romans left untouched. Berbers practiced various religious rites without a common idol or God to worship. Around A.D. 100, Romans banished Jews from what is now Europe to North Africa after their revolt in other parts of the empire. Many Berbers, including whole groups, converted to Judaism.

Within a century Christianity gained a foothold in the Jewish community and won converts among the slaves and in larger towns. By A.D. 313, Emperor Constantine I adopted Christianity as the official religion of the Roman Empire, which included much of North Africa.

Berber political protest against Rome now took the form of religious opposition. Groups of nonbelievers gained support against religious purists in the Roman Catholic church. Saint Augustine, bishop of Hippo, earned recognition as an author and

Left: St. Augustine, bishop of Hippo
Right: The Vandals took what they wanted from the land and then moved on.

outspoken critic of freethinkers around 400. His sermons and books called for early separation of church and state, an idea he believed would save souls should Rome fall.

VANDAL AND BYZANTINE RULE

Rome eventually did weaken and fall to a Germanic tribe, called the Vandals, who swept through southern Europe. In 429 the cruel warrior, Gaiseric, continued Vandal looting across the Mediterranean to defeat Roman armies from Tangiers eastward. Once in Carthage, merciless Gaiseric settled to rule his kingdom. The fifty thousand Vandals in his army were said to be so ruthless that the word *vandalism* became a term for recklessness and destruction.

Unlike Romans, Vandals had little interest in influencing the people they conquered. They only settled in areas that would bring them riches. They took what they could from the land and

Belisarius, a Byzantine general, vowed to drive the Vandals out of North Africa. In this engraving Belisarius presents captive Vandal chiefs to Emperor Justinian.

abandoned the rest to decay. Vandals left local government to Romans. But as Arian Christians (who rejected the doctrine of the Holy Trinity), they fought to destroy the influence of the Roman Catholic church. Anyone clinging to Christianity had their tongues and hands cut off. Others escaped to Spain.

Gradually, Vandals made North Africa their home. They intermarried with urban Phoenicians, Berbers, and Romans and lost some of their fight. After one hundred years the Vandal kingdom fell to a Byzantine general, Belisarius. Belisarius's goal was to drive the Vandals out of North Africa in order to revive the Roman Empire.

Byzantine rule restored much of the order, but little of the prosperity lost under the Vandals. Roman clergy returned with their Christianity. However, so did Berber resentment toward Roman authority and the Catholic church. Byzantine rule for the next one hundred years never had the same control over Berbers as earlier. Mountain Berbers and Sahara nomads, in particular, looked to their chieftains for protection once again.

Muhammad, the prophet who spread the religion of Islam

CONQUERING ARABS

The most lasting impact on Berber culture came from widespread Arab invasions in the seventh and eleventh centuries.

Arabs who once worshiped idols followed the teachings of the religious prophet, Muhammad. Muhammad believed in a single all-powerful God, Allah, whose laws were above those of individual, family, and government. The Arabic word *Islam* means "submission." Therefore, followers of Islam became known as *Muslims*, people who "submit to God's will."

By the time Muhammad died in 632, he had converted much of the Arabian Peninsula to his reform religion of Islam. After his death, Muslim armies swept across North Africa to bring the word of Allah to the Western world.

Muslim military easily triumphed over the Byzantine colonies. However, Berbers stubbornly opposed Arab takeover. Legend states that a female chieftain, Al-Kahina, led the first flickers of resistance in eastern Algeria. Under Al-Kahina's direction Berbers fought Arab invaders for several years in the Aurès Mountains before dying in battle. Centuries later Algerian rebellion for independence from France would begin at this same location.

Soon all of North Africa was under Arab rule, and the Muslims pressed toward Spain. Many converted Berbers assisted the Muslims. Arabs that stayed settled in Algeria's urban areas, many taking Berber wives. Over time, townspeople and farmers converted to Islam. Nomads also became Muslims. But for many, religion lasted as long as the army, tax collector, or slave trader stayed. Berbers rejected the laws of Islam, or *sharia*, and clung to tribal government. Moreover, they denied the idea that religious leaders, or *caliphs*, could be Arabian Muslims only.

Similar to Roman times, rebellion against Arab control came in the form of heretical religious sects. The most widespread movement, the Kharidjites, began in Morocco in 739. Kharidjites claimed that any Muslim, without regard to race, could become caliph. This belief in equality brought Berber support from throughout the Maghrib.

The Kharidjites revolt led to creation of many smaller kingdoms. The groups accepted Islam but rejected Arab rule. Of these kingdoms, the Rustumid Dynasty from Tahirt earned the reputation for the fairest leaders and most learned people. Rustumid governors were known for the study of mathematics, astronomy, law, and religion—to the neglect of their military.

The Fatimids Dynasty, named after Muhammad's daughter Fatima, overthrew the Kharidjites and claimed central Maghrib in the name of their form of Islam in 911. Some Kharidjites escaped southward into the desert, where their descendants still live.

Even with their religious zeal, early Arab missionaries were only a small privileged group within urban Maghrib. However, a second wave of Arab nomads from southwest Arabia, the Hililians, changed the entire face of North Africa extending to

A Moorish warrior

Spain. Hililians swarmed inland over the countryside to uproot farmers and plunder their pastures. To survive, Berbers either joined their conquerors as nomads or fled to the mountains. Many Berbers began to adopt Arab culture, language, and religion.

Two great empires formed to govern the Maghrib and Spain for the next two hundred years. The Almoravids, from 1042 to 1147, and Almohads, from 1147 to 1269, instilled a common Berber culture.

In Spain, Berber Muslims were called Moors. Moors blended refined artistic tastes from Spain with Berber might. Moorish influence spanned eastward from Spain across the Maghrib. Elegant Moorish architecture still remains at the Grand Mosque of Tlemcen and in other major Algerian cities.

Arab conquest grew too large geographically for one power to control by horseback or boat. Conflict within the Almohad Dynasty led to renewed warfare. Without support the dynasty crumbled. Muslim power waned, but not before transforming North Africa into a population of "Arabized Berbers."

Chapter 3

HIDDEN ALGERIA

BRIEF RETURN OF CHRISTIANITY

Christian kingdoms took advantage of the infighting. Their armies pressed into Spain until the city of Granada fell in 1492, marking the end of Muslim rule. Spanish Christians demanded that Muslims convert to Christianity and that Jews be expelled. Thousands of people from Spain fled to North Africa rather than convert. Those who remained without converting were tortured and burned.

Meanwhile, Spain sought to extend its commercial interests. Christian militia seized North African ports along the Mediterranean. By 1510, Spain captured the most useful ports of Mers el Kebir, Oran, Bougie, and Algiers. News of Spain's violent attacks and savage treatment of local citizens spread throughout coastal communities. Those Algerian ports yet unvisited by Spanish warships pleaded with Spain's King Ferdinand to let them pay tribute, or taxes, rather than be subdued also.

Piracy was always a problem throughout the Mediterranean. However, hatred for Spain provoked its growth. Islamic Ottoman Turks and Christian outlaws saw piracy against ships from

Khair al Din was called Barbarossa, or Redbeard.

Christian countries as a way to continue the holy war against Christianity *and* get rich. Piracy became big business between the sixteenth and nineteenth centuries.

PIRACY REIGNS

Near Algiers, Spain controlled the seas from a rocky offshore island fort they called Penon. From here, Spain extracted tolls and interfered with commerce. Angry local merchants invited two bold pirate brothers, Arudj and Khair al Din, to oust the Spaniards. Spain's Penon troops successfully fought off the pirates. Still, the brothers captured Algiers and made it their central base for piracy and inland conquests.

At first, the elder Arudj commanded Algiers. After his death at the hands of the pro-Spanish ruler at Tlemcen, Khair al Din took charge. Barbarossa, or Redbeard as Europeans called Khair al Din, knew that the threat from Spain and the discontent of the Algiers citizens were great. So he swore allegiance to the Turkish sultan in exchange for Ottoman protection.

The alliance proved profitable. The Ottoman Empire had extensive land forces. They built Barbarossa sleek swift vessels that easily could overtake clumsy European merchant ships. Barbarossa's naval skills outdistanced all others. With ships and Turkish troops, Barbarossa established Ottoman rule along the coast from Constantine to Oran and finally overtook Penon in 1529.

Algiers became the center of Ottoman rule in the Maghrib. Turks extended the name "Algiers" to mean the entire area around the city. Originally it came from the Arabic word *el jazair*, referring to its harbor islands. Turks called the area "Algeria" and the Turkish people living there "Algerians." Turkish became the official language of government, a government that prohibited Arab and Berber representation. Berbers who protested were cruelly crushed. The one concession Turks made to Berbers was to call the territory the Turks conquered Barbary states after the Berbers.

The Turkish sultan appointed Barbarossa *beylerbey*, or commander in chief, of Algiers. Under Barbarossa the port became the seat of Muslim piracy. Even after Barbarossa left Algiers to be captain of the Ottoman fleet in 1533, his successful military and government machinery continued with a series of powerful pirates.

For three centuries under the Turks, no Christian ship was safe on the Mediterranean. Privateering captains, or *rais*, boarded Christian vessels, stole their cargo, and enslaved the crews. Wealthy captives usually were held for ransom. Most other captives either wound up as slaves at auction or on ship crews. As long as tribute was paid to the sultan, adventurers were left alone.

Captains lived well off their bounty. They dressed in ornate clothes and inhabited grand fortresses. Their homes overflowed with spoils from Europe and the Orient, including riches, a harem, and slaves as servants.

Barbary pirate raids swelled the purses of the Ottoman Empire and became Algeria's main source of income. By the seventeenth century the slave population in Algiers alone was said to have reached thirty thousand. Slave trading was so much a part of the city's economy that Christians were dissuaded from converting to Islam so they would remain captive.

Captains organized their thriving businesses into *taifas*, or guilds. These unions gave captains a stronger voice in local government to guard and promote their trade interests. Tyrannical captains took over ports and asserted authority. They governed as *deys*, or representatives of the sultan's government.

Pirates constantly fought each other. Nonetheless, daily local government ran fairly smooth. As throughout the Ottoman Empire, each ethnic group had guild representation. Turks, Berbers, Arabs, and Jews were governed by their own people. In the countryside, chieftains kept allegiance of their clans. Groups that paid their taxes were left alone. Although commerce and city improvements dwindled under the Turks, life for the average Algerian changed little.

BARBARY WARS

By the eighteenth century the Barbary pirates were unmanageable. European naval fleets now paid hefty tolls for safe passage through Mediterranean waters. In 1797, the United States negotiated a twelve-year treaty with the dey of Algiers that paid a tribute of $10 million for protection of American ships. As with

Left: A galley of the Barbary pirates
Right: Commodore Stephen Decatur meets with the dey of Algiers.

similar deals, the untrustworthy thieves accepted payment but continued to seize ships and enslave sailors.

The United States finally fought back in crushing raids that became known as the Barbary Wars. In 1815 Commodore Stephen Decatur, with ten warships, seized several pirate vessels. Then he attacked the port of Algiers with blazing guns until the dey promised to leave American ships alone and pay for past damages. As happened before, the treaty was short-lived. The following year, however, British admiral Viscount Edward Exmouth fired on Algiers until the dey agreed to end revenge against Christians.

FRENCH CONQUEST

Many European countries looked toward expanding their borders in the early 1800s. For France, the time was right. King Charles X believed that adding new colonies would distract the French people from his troubled regime.

Left: Charles X   Right: The French take over the city of Algiers

On April 29, 1827, the perfect opportunity presented itself. Dey Hussein of Algiers met with the French consul to urge payment of a thirty-year unpaid bill for Algerian wheat. The French claimed that payment depended upon Algeria's promise to stop pirating. Dey Hussein became so angry he struck the French consul with a flyswatter. Then he called him "a wicked, faithless, idol-worshiping rascal."

King Charles demanded a public apology. When none came, he ordered a blockade of Algerian ports. For three years Dey Hussein essentially ignored the blockade. Charles grew weary of the delay. On June 14, 1830, he ordered thirty-seven thousand French troops to the coastal town of Sidi Ferruch, thirteen miles (twenty-one kilometers) west of Algiers. Three weeks later, French soldiers marched into Algiers, overthrew the city, and exiled the dey. July 5, 1830 marked the end of piracy in North Africa and the beginning of many years of suffering under French rule. For the next 132 years, Algerians would still live in a country that belonged to someone else.

Louis Philippe   Abd al Qadir

FRENCH COLONIZATION

At first, France was unsure of what to do with its new conquest. Louis Philippe had dethroned Charles, and French liberals opposed further campaigns. Other French argued for expansion.

After much bickering, Louis Philippe declared the territory a French colony in 1834. He set Algeria's modern borders and appointed a governor-general to carry out legal, military, and civic duties.

With colonial government in place along the coast, the French were ready to expand inland. However, occupation of the interior proved difficult. Arab groups fiercely opposed French settlers, or *colons*. Resistance quickly took the form of a holy war. Islamic purists fought what they called pagan Christian French under the leadership of Abd al Qadir.

Abd al Qadir became one of the most important freedom fighters in Algerian history. As self-proclaimed "Sultan of the

General Thomas Bugeaud rides through a conquered Arab village.

Arabs,'' he united warring Algerians and battled the French for fifteen years. He organized territories unoccupied by the French into a strong Muslim state supported by an army, taxes, educational system, public works, and merchant groups.

Abd al Qadir led almost all Arabs from central and western Algeria by 1840. His successes interfered with further French settlement. France answered this Muslim threat by sending tough General Thomas Bugeaud and reinforcement troops to defeat Abd al Qadir's forces. Bugeaud's methods were brutal—destroying villages, burning crops, killing herds, and setting fires at cave openings where Arab families hid. By 1847, the French army outnumbered the Arabs by 100,000 soldiers.

Slowly, Bugeaud pushed back the Arabs. Village after village fell to the French. Accepting the loss, Abd al Qadir surrendered to French authorities in December 1847. His defeat meant the loss of freedom and land for the Algerian people.

Abd al Qadir spent the next four years in a French prison. The next French administration, under Napoleon III, allowed Abd al Qadir to resettle in Damascus, Syria. In 1860 Abd al Qadir earned the French Legion of Honor award from his former enemies. He had saved twelve thousand Christians, including French officials, from slaughter by local Turks. Otherwise, he kept out of public life, devoting the rest of his life to study and to the poor.

To Algerians, Abd al Qadir will always be a hero. Abd al Qadir's banner became the national flag after the war of independence. On the fourth anniversary of Algerian independence on July 5, 1966, Algerians erected a mosque dedicated to Abd al Qadir in Constantine as a national shrine.

THE RISE OF FRENCH ALGERIA

France tried to deprive Algerians of their country and their culture. First, France successfully enticed settlers to Algeria from throughout Europe. When French troops landed, there were 5,000 Europeans in Algeria out of 3 million people. By 1881 over 300,000 Europeans, 50 percent French, had emigrated to central North Africa, where there were now barely 2.5 million Arabs.

Second, France automatically granted colons French citizenship. Algerians could gain citizenship only after renouncing their Islamic religion. The French missionary, Father Charles Foucauld, best described colonial policy: "If we cannot succeed in making Frenchmen of these people, they will drive us out. The only way to make them into Frenchmen is to make them Christians."

Desert Arabs killed Father Foucauld by the end of the nineteenth century. Most Arabs refused Christianity, grasping instead to the few rituals the French could not take away, such as hiding Arab women behind veils. The few Arabs that became French citizens were branded traitors to Islam.

The great influx of colons and repressive French laws caused colons, aided by French military, to gain control of the government, business, culture, and land. Algerians became despised second-class citizens in their own country.

Colons flocked wherever there was water and fertile land. France seized whole stretches of former Turkish, tribal, and private property and sold it to Europeans. At one point, free tracts of land were given to any settler who promised to improve the land. After shady land deals, colons converted the wilderness to rich coastal farmland and introduced modern technology—all at Berber expense.

Then Napoleon III visited Algeria in the 1860s. He was so impressed with the dignity of the beaten chieftains and greed of the colons that he reversed his policy and halted European expansion beyond the coast. New law recognized Arab group ownership of religious land. But the law was poorly enforced, and it turned out to be too little too late.

Often poor and landless, Algerians left their villages to find work. But jobs were scarce. Some Muslims were forced to join the military. Many Algerians became laborers for starvation wages on what was their own land. A few found work for colons in overcrowded cities. Unemployment in cities soared. Sometimes, only women of the household could find jobs, as servants, to support the family.

Deprived of work, language, and cultural heritage, many Algerians retreated to the protection of Islam and a dream of independent Algeria. But groups were too scattered to organize against the French. Sporadic revolts were quickly crushed.

The largest revolt since Abd al Qadir began in the Kabylie Mountains and spread throughout Algeria in 1871. Mohammed el Hadj Mokrani led Muslim farmers frustrated by military refusal to give them seed to grow crops. Three years before the riot, almost 20 percent of the Muslim population of Constantine starved due to French agricultural policies.

France stifled the uprising and moved to punish all Muslims. The French governor seized more tribal land. He tightened controls on tribal government and the already limited Muslim education system, Arab travel, and meeting in groups. Muslims were politically, socially, and economically silenced. With these restrictions, France crippled the tribal system and destroyed the single organized voice for negotiation.

DAWN OF ALGERIAN NATIONALISM

Between World War I and World War II, a new generation of Arab emerged in Algeria. Almost 200,000 Muslims entered the French army and 25,000 died in battle. Hundreds of thousands more assisted the war effort by working in French factories. These men observed freedom under democratic politics. They experienced a higher standard of living than was possible at home. Traveling outside Algeria they felt the undertone of Arab nationalism building throughout the Middle East.

At first, Arab reformers called for equality. But colons opposed any reform that might interfere with their privileged status. After World War I France rewarded Arab loyalty with limited Arab representation in local government and citizenship to select Arab groups. These attempts to tip the scales of power actually provided minimal gains. Defeat of one reform bill after another in

France fueled the flames for a separate Algerian nation and an Arab Algeria.

The first group to call for independence from France was the Star of North Africa in 1926. The group's leader, Messali Hadj, organized Algerian workers in France. He demanded a separate country and military, and the right to vote. As his group gained support, the French government banned it and imprisoned Messali for being anti-French. In 1937, Messali returned to Algeria to rally urban workers and peasant farmers to the same anticolonist causes. He saw Islam as a bond between the people in their collective struggle for independence. Colons declared Messali's second group, the Party of the Algerian People, illegal in the mid-1930s and jailed him again.

About the same time, other groups developed—some advocating political and economic equality under French rule and some calling for a separate nation that embraced strict Islamic teachings, Arabic language, and Algerian homeland. But with each failed attempt to win rights from the French came greater accord in the push for a Muslim Algeria. And each movement brought more French repression and threats from fearful colons.

THE WAR YEARS

Initially, Algerian Muslims fought with the French in World War II as they did in the First World War. Then German Nazis occupied northern France. A cooperative French-German government, called the Vichy regime, was established to govern southern France and French colonies such as Algeria.

Most colons supported the regime. But Muslims objected to Nazi policies. Germans stripped Algerian Jews of their French

Left: General Charles de Gaulle, photographed in 1944
Right: United States soldiers landing near Oran in 1942

citizenship and arrested Muslim and European opposition leaders. On November 8, 1942, seventy thousand British and American troops landed at Algiers and Oran. Three days later the Vichy government surrendered. Algeria became an Allied base of operations for the rest of the war.

Exiled French military requested that Muslims join Allied armies. A new leader for independence, Ferhat Abbas, responded with a manifesto to the Algerian people. The manifesto, which was signed by 56 anticolonialist leaders, demanded an Algerian constitution guaranteeing equality for Muslims in return for service. General Charles de Gaulle, leader of the Free France movement, only partly answered the demands. His response to grant 60,000 selected Muslims French citizenship was not enough. Instead, Abbas and other Muslims, including Messali, formed Friends of the Manifesto and Liberty (AML) to work for Algerian liberation. Within a year the group claimed 500,000 supporters.

By May 8, 1945, the day war ended in Europe, tension between Muslims and colons exploded. Thousands of Muslims organized by the AML marched into the streets of Setif to celebrate victory. Many carried illegal posters saying "Long Live Free and Independent Algeria" and "We Want to Be Your Equals," and green and white flags that would become symbols of the liberation movement. French police grabbed the banners. Shots rang out. Soon riots were everywhere. Marchers raged through the streets, killing Europeans as they went. As word spread of a holy war, protest ignited in other cities.

Police, civil vigilantes, and the military responded with their own violence. The lucky Algerians were arrested and jailed. Others were executed or buried in common graves. When the smoke cleared, the French reported 103 Europeans dead at Setif. Estimates of the number of Muslims who died varied from 1,300 to 15,000. Open revolution was years away, but lines were sharply drawn at Setif.

The French government tried to calm the worsening political situation. But every step forward seemed like two backward. Colons resented any Arab gains. Arabs felt the French never gave enough. Muslims wanted to end the two-college system of government that gave 500,000 colons much greater voice than 9 million Muslims. Colons feared they would "drown in a Muslim sea" with any government changes. When elections opened slightly, colons made sure they were rigged. Frustration with the spineless French government and hostility toward colons convinced Algerians that violence was their only recourse for change.

Many groups prepared for revolt. Messali, fresh from five years in a French prison, organized a new party called the Movement

Ahmed Ben Bella (above)
Gamal Abdel Nasser (right)

for the Triumph of Democratic Liberties (MTLD). This group
sought absolute independence through political channels. A secret
Special Organization (OS) within MTLD executed terrorist attacks
against colons. By 1952, OS violence led to Messali's arrest and
expulsion to France. This time, Messali remained in France until
his death in 1974, leaving the fight for nationalism to fresh
leadership.

After Messali left, his groups became divided. Ahmed Ben Bella,
an OS leader, formed a new underground organization based in
Cairo, Egypt. Here Ben Bella and eight other original members
from the Revolutionary Committee of Unity and Action planned
the Algerian revolution. They became known as the historic
chiefs.

For eight months in 1954, the group established their military
network in Algeria. Egyptian president Gamal Abdel Nasser
helped organize foreign assistance for the revolt, including arms,
money, and supplies. In October the group renamed its political
arm the National Liberation Front (FLN). The military arm,
National Liberation Army (ALN), led the fight for independence
within Algeria.

Chapter 4

BIRTH OF MODERN
ALGERIA

THE REVOLUTION

On November 1, 1954, All Saints' Day, ALN guerrillas attacked key military and communication posts throughout northern Algeria. At the same time the FLN broadcast their message from Cairo. They called on Muslims to "join the national struggle for restoration of the Algerian state . . . within the framework of the principles of Islam."

French response was quick. François Mitterrand, French interior minister, declared that "the only possible negotiation is war." France sent its best paratroopers to crush the initial rebellion in the Aurès Mountains. Even so, the revolt spread southeast to the forested mountains around Constantine. The large French military had difficulty withstanding fierce guerrilla attacks on soldiers, Europeans, and Muslims who cooperated with France. Within a year the French knew they had full-scale revolution.

Fighting was violent on all sides. Outnumbered in battle, Muslims pursued a savage course of guerrilla warfare that included ambushes, night raids, kidnapping, and torture. One trademark of their terrorism was the Kabyle smile, or slit throat.

The ALN parades in front of its officers (above).
French soldiers frisk Algerians in a raid on Algiers (right).

As the ALN fanned the countryside, many colon farmers fled to Algiers for protection. By 1958, colons organized, too. Vigilante groups hunted down FLN members and often killed Muslims at will. Colons forming political pressure groups demanded that the French governor restore peace and punish outlaw nationalists.

In response, France committed nearly half a million troops to defending one million colons and controlling nine million Muslims. They built 200 miles (322 kilometers) of border barriers to keep guerrillas in Tunisia and Morocco from crossing into Algeria. To avenge losses, the French conducted massive searches to destroy ALN strongholds. They bombed villages, burned Muslim crops, and tortured prisoners. Before the revolution ended, they had forced about three million Arabs into prisons or guarded relocation camps.

FLN gains were significantly greater in the world arena than in battle. News of French cruelty reached the United Nations after

After becoming premier of France, de Gaulle still did not want to give Algeria independence.

French troops brutally raked the city for FLN members in the Battle of Algiers. Soon there was international pressure for Algerian nationalism. As far away as the United States, Senator John F. Kennedy proclaimed his disagreement with United States policy supporting France in North Africa.

Within France, the war took its toll. The country was being torn apart over what to do with Algeria. Between 1954 and 1958, the French people saw the rise and fall of six governments. In 1958, Charles de Gaulle's election confirmed the policy that Algeria remain French. Only military and colons were satisfied.

De Gaulle's first acts were to propose reforms for improving Muslim conditions in exchange for a cease-fire. The FLN flatly refused any settlement short of total independence. Bloodshed on both sides soared to new heights. Muslim and colon terrorist activities reached the streets of Paris.

By 1961, war-weary de Gaulle reversed his policy. He promised

Algerian Muslims their own nation if they voted for independence. Feeling betrayed, colons and military rioted in the streets of Algiers, capturing government buildings and bombing public places. Their terrorist campaign, called the Secret Army Organization (OAS), was directed from Algiers by retired French officer, Raoul Salan. Between FLN and OAS battering, France was close to civil war.

INDEPENDENCE

Talks broke off and reopened several times after de Gaulle came to power. Negotiations were complicated by France's desire to hold on to oil and natural gas in the Sahara desert. Finally, France and the FLN signed an agreement on March 18, 1962. A cease-fire would begin the next day. The vote for independence would be July 1.

Despite raging OAS terrorism, Algerians overwhelmingly voted for independence. On July 3, Charles de Gaulle declared Algeria a free nation. However, revolutionary leaders officially declared Independence Day on July 5, 1962, 132 years after the French had captured Algiers.

BUILDING FREE ALGERIA

Postwar Algeria was in shambles. The economy toppled after colons fled during and after the revolution. The only semblance of government was the exiled FLN leadership. Once in Algeria, rival FLN factions competed for power. But all the people wanted were decent jobs, secure housing, and an education. As civil war loomed closer, they cried, "Seven years, that's enough!"

Ben Bella (left) and Colonel Houari Boumediene

On September 20, 1962, there was an election for the Algerian National Assembly. The FLN formally transferred its power to the Democratic and Popular Republic of Algeria. Ahmed Ben Bella, with military strength from ALN chief of staff Colonel Houari Boumediene, gained a political edge on his opponents. Six days later the assembly elected him premier. In turn, Ben Bella rewarded Boumediene with the post of defense minister.

Within a year a new constitution was approved by popular vote, and Ben Bella assumed the presidency for five years. Under its guidelines, Arabic became Algeria's official language and Islam the country's religion. In addition, the constitution gave Ben Bella authority as supreme commander of the armed forces and head of the Supreme Court. Ben Bella assumed the position of general secretary of the FLN, Algeria's only political party, giving him control of all government, military, and political decision making.

One of the first tasks of government was to ease the terrible economic situation. Colons had been the skilled workers and administrators. They were the doctors, teachers, and engineers France never allowed Muslims to become. Once colons left, factories and farms ceased to operate, leaving 70 percent of the population unemployed. With many villages destroyed, there were thousands of poor, homeless, and sick Algerians.

In March 1963, Ben Bella authorized a series of laws called the March Decrees. These laws permitted takeover of vacant property left by colons. The state became owner of the richest farmland, factories, mines, banks, transportation system, and retail stores. To run these projects, the state devised a system of worker self-management known as *autogestion*. Public ownership of property became the basis for Algeria's brand of socialism.

At first, Ben Bella's reforms moved slowly. Then he made radical changes to consolidate his power within the military, FLN, and government. Ben Bella soon extended his influence internationally, declaring himself spokesperson for political independence from industrialized nations.

To Algerians, Ben Bella paid more attention to foreign affairs than to issues at home. Local district leaders and the military feared his vast power. Many thought him a dictator. Even his closest allies, like Boumediene, were disturbed. In June 1965, the army turned against Ben Bella in a bloodless coup. The ousted president was arrested and his former supporter, Boumediene, took command.

A NEW REGIME

Compared to Ben Bella's confused politics, Boumediene provided low-key reform. Boumediene's government sought to replace Ben Bella's one person rule with organized state agencies. He claimed Ben Bella's ideals, but with greater emphasis on improving Algerian life without impressing other countries.

Boumediene's first acts were to suspend the 1963 constitution, reduce FLN power, and transfer authority from the National Assembly to a twenty-six-member Council of the Revolution, a military-based body. Initially, there was some dissent from Ben Bella's supporters. Once they quieted, Boumediene set about restructuring local politics and the economy.

In May 1969, the government held elections for representatives of *wilayas*, or administrative districts. Boumediene decentralized government further by dividing the nation into smaller communes. Each commune elected a popular assembly. Anyone over eighteen could vote. But only FLN party members could run for the assembly.

Despite increased local representation, Boumediene wanted greater public voice in political decision making. On his tenth anniversary as president, Boumediene announced creation of a national charter and constitution. The national charter went through surprisingly extensive public debate at local meetings and in the media before its approval on June 27, 1976. The charter's passage reinforced Algeria's Socialist character, a commitment to Islam, and confidence in Boumediene.

The constitution of November 1976 established the National Popular Assembly, a legislature elected by the people and approved by the party, and a Council of Ministers who were appointed by the president. It called for elected popular assemblies at the community level and in the forty-eight wilayas. The next month the FLN overwhelmingly selected Boumediene as president.

Some Algerians protested that Boumediene's changes only added an inefficient bureaucracy. However, Boumediene's political reorganization proved more successful than his economic program. Between 1968 and 1972 Boumediene focused on rapidly developing oil and gas production in order to generate revenue for other industry. Seventy percent of Algerian investments went for industrialization. Only 15 percent went into agriculture. The plan did little to lower high unemployment rates and keep unemployed farm workers from flocking to urban areas.

Since his takeover, Boumediene had advocated assuming control of foreign-owned businesses in Algeria. In 1971, he launched his first four-year plan for industrial independence, and nationalized the French oil companies. Unlike Ben Bella, Boumediene encouraged diplomatic and trade relations with Algeria's former enemy. France wanted to buy Algerian oil now, and Algeria needed French money.

At the same time, the government realized the need to increase Algeria's ability to feed its own people. Boumediene's agricultural revolution redistributed public land to rural peasants for cooperative farms. New villages improved living standards. Yet, food shortages and worker migration continued to be a problem.

FOREIGN POLICY

After liberation, Algeria sought a place in the world arena. Its causes were those of other Africans, Arabs, and nationalist movements similar to the fight for Algerian nationhood.

By the end of 1962, Algeria received membership in the Arab League and United Nations. The following year Algeria became a founding member of the Organization of African Unity (OAU), a

In 1976 Boumediene became president.

group promoting African causes. Algeria often has used the OAU to support the Palestine Liberation Organization (PLO) in its fight for statehood against Israel and to condemn the racist white minority in South Africa.

Under Boumediene, Algerian policy was to remain separate from all major powers. Boumediene wanted poorer nations to have the same voice as richer nations in world matters. He saw high-priced natural resources as a political tool for developing countries to gain wealth and equality. After the Arab-Israeli War in 1973, Algeria was one of the fifteen Arab countries to raise oil prices and suspend shipment to Western countries supporting Israel.

Closer to home, Algeria gave shelter, weapons, and money to the Polisario (Popular Front for the Liberation of Saguia el Hamra and Rio de Oro), a guerrilla group claiming rights to the Western Sahara, a former Spanish colony. Spain gave joint administration of the area to Morocco and Mauritania in 1976. But the Saharawis,

The funeral procession of President Houari Boumediene

who live in the desert, armed for independence and set up an exile government in Algiers.

Algeria broke relations with its two neighbors over Polisario struggles, but reestablished relations with Mauritania after it surrendered claims to the area. Still, Moroccan-Algerian relations remained strained over this and other border disputes. Someday Algeria hopes to cement relations for political and economic unity by forming a union called the "Greater Maghrib" with Tunisia, Morocco, Mauritania, Libya, and Western Sahara.

Under Boumediene, Algeria became a leader in the Arab world and a voice for Third World nations. Official recognition of world influence came when the United Nations General Assembly elected Algerian foreign minister, Abdel Aziz Bouteflika, as president in 1974. For the first time, developing nations had leverage as a united force against the will of the United States and the Soviet Union.

PRESIDENT FOR THE 80s

On December 27, 1978, Boumediene died suddenly of a rare blood disease. Within a month FLN party delegates met to

President and First Lady Benjedid

nominate Colonel Chadli Benjedid as president. On February 7, 1979, Benjedid became Algeria's third president, for a five-year term.

Benjedid moved quickly to change many Boumediene policies and gain public support. As a way to weed out Boumediene holdovers, Benjedid launched a large-scale anticorruption drive against public figures. After appointing a new prime minister and Council of Ministers, he lifted restrictions, such as the hated exit travel visa, and released political prisoners, including Ben Bella.

Two main thrusts of Benjedid's government were to open the economy for greater opportunity and to concentrate on agricultural development. To reduce mismanagement, Benjedid broke up large government-owned businesses and farms into more manageable size. And he opened the Algerian economy to limited foreign investment.

With Benjedid, Algeria's high profile in Third World affairs took a back seat to improving the economy at home. Still, Algeria kept its international role as peaceful "bridge builder." In the 1980s, the Algerian government negotiated disputes between Iran and Iraq, Syria and Jordan, and factions within Lebanon. The United States saw the successful return of embassy hostages due to Algerian intervention with Iran in 1981.

In January 1984 and December 1988, Benjedid was elected to a second and later third five-year term as president. Even with sweeping reforms, Benjedid holds a tight rein on the government. The revised FLN power structure gave Benjedid primary policy-making authority in addition to control of major government, business, and party appointments.

Benjedid's policies reflected the same revolutionary principles of Arab identity as advocated since independence. However, university students, devout Muslims, and ethnic Berbers sometimes challenged Benjedid's policies for diverse reasons. In October 1988, a week of riots erupted in most major towns. Angry unemployed youth protested the lack of jobs and food, housing shortages, and unequal distribution of wealth. Some held that elite government employees abused their power. Raging young men destroyed symbols of private government wealth. Police moved to crush the disturbances. When police stopped firing, the death toll reached almost 250. Three thousand Algerians were arrested and large parts of Algiers and other cities were in ruins.

Benjedid first acted to restore order. Then he made new appointments and granted concessions that would reshape and liberalize Algeria's future. Changes in the constitution shifted some powers to the prime minister, who was made responsible to the Algerian Popular Assembly. Additional reforms allowed

*Devastation in 1988 caused by riots over rising
prices and a government austerity plan.*

candidates from outside the FLN to run for legislature. However,
Benjedid's boldest constitutional reform was the creation of a
multiparty system that guaranteed greater individual freedoms.

Algeria has come a long way since independence. But the
maturing country continues to grapple with its identity in the
modern industrialized world. Algeria's leaders accept the
challenge of reform. Only time will tell whether they can quiet the
unrest and lead Algeria into full adulthood.

A busy commercial section of the city of Constantine

Chapter 5

ALGERIANS BUILD A MODERN WORLD

Government and economy go hand in hand in Algeria. Since independence, there has been a conscious effort to bring production and distribution under state direction.

In the beginning, the young government was forced to control the economy. Once Algeria merely served as provider of raw materials to a colonial master. Without French management, technical expertise, and money, Algeria had to assume responsibility for its disorganized and underskilled economy. The new nation saw a modern, developed economy as a way to remain independent and satisfy people's basic needs.

Soon the government's presence reached into every economic arena. The state controlled most industry, modern agriculture, local trade, all banking, and foreign trade. At the local level, the government organized Socialist worker management committees to run farms and factories. The central government decided how the economy should grow and what direction it should take. Every few years the ministry of finance reevaluated progress and formulated a revised multiyear development plan to follow.

The oil industry initially raised Algeria's standard of living. The thriving oil well at the left was photographed in 1958. A modern oil and gas port, with a refinery in the background (above)

Initially, there was to be a three-stage program for rapidly industrializing the economy. Funding for heavy industry, like steel and iron production, in the first stage was to come from expanded gas and oil profits.

At first, oil and gas brought enough money to raise the standard of living. Algeria quickly took its place in the world market as a country determined to manage its own affairs. It provided social services for its people, borrowed little, and invested a great deal.

But Algerian industry mainly provided jobs for skilled labor. Unskilled jobs for most of Algeria's work force were limited since French factories closed. Agriculture, too, lagged behind because of lack of funding and attention to modernization. More and more food and supplies for daily living needed to be imported. Poor farmers swamped cities in search of jobs.

When oil profits slumped in the early 1980s, unemployment soared, inflation skyrocketed, and shortages developed of such staples as eggs and cooking oil. The government responded with changes to revive the failing economy. Large bureaucratic farm and industry collectives were broken into smaller, more manageable units.

In one of its boldest reforms, Algeria opened investment to more private and foreign participation. The economy refocused upon educating, training, and employing unskilled workers on farms and in industries that would make Algeria less dependent upon other nations for everyday goods.

NATURAL RESOURCES

Algeria's most valuable natural resources are clearly oil and natural gas. The French first discovered large oil deposits in 1956 near Hassi Messaoud in the Eastern Sahara and gas in 1958 near Hassi R'Mel in the northwestern Sahara.

Soon after independence, the French worked out an arrangement whereby they retained part of their investment in oil production. Algeria needed foreign money and talent to explore and refine its resources.

Most oil and gas firms, however, became nationalized under a government agency called SONATRACH. SONATRACH explored for minerals, built pipelines, and exported products to foreign countries. Small towns sprouted around main oil refineries in Skikda, Arzew, Hassi Messaoud, and In Amenas. Major pipelines linked oil fields to ports along the coast. Algeria and Italy constructed the first trans-Mediterranean pipeline through Tunisia.

Within ten years of its formation in 1963, SONATRACH became one of the larger oil-producing companies in the world. In

The port of Oran (above) and
a workman cutting cork (left)

1982 the government divided SONATRACH into thirteen separate companies as part of a decentralization program. In addition, the new program allowed private, foreign, and domestic investment.

When world demand for oil declined, so did OPEC (Organization of Petroleum Exporting Countries) — and Algerian — prices. Algeria cut back on production in the mid-1980s and switched to natural gas production, as the resource with the greatest growth potential. Algeria ranked fourth in the world supply of natural gas, exporting large amounts to Japan, North America, and Western Europe. By 1989, oil and gas combined made up about 30 percent of Algeria's economic production.

More recently, Algerians explored rich supplies of nonfuel minerals. Mercury, phosphate, and iron ore were used at home and exported abroad. Although quantities were small, they were relatively large compared with other countries. Algerian mines produced 12 percent of the world's mercury. Algeria also is one of a few countries to yield barite, which is used in paper manufacture, and fuller's earth, a filtering mineral.

The 1985-89 development plan allocated funds to develop these nonfuel resources further. It also cited forestry as an area for expansion of resources. Algeria is one of the major cork producers in the world.

MANUFACTURING

Until recently, industrial development received priority over agricultural development. Most funding went to expanding basic industries utilizing resources of oil, iron, and steel. Government emphasized "industrializing industry." This meant manufacturing heavy agricultural, manufacturing, and construction equipment rather than food products, clothing, or household goods.

Workers at an olive press

This policy had problems from the start. Like the oil industry, heavy industry required fewer, more skilled workers. Young Algeria clearly lacked the skilled labor to compete in the modern market. Production output was low and the quality poor.

In the early 1980s, the government moved to stimulate industry. Money for industry supported more products that consumers craved. These also were industries that utilized greater numbers of unskilled laborers. Considerable growth took place in manufacture of plastics, fertilizer, paper, clothing, leather goods, and food. Production of building materials and electronics increased greatly. About two-thirds of the country's output came from national companies. And almost one-third of the workers found jobs in the industry.

Large sums of money went into factory construction. "Work and rigor to assure the future" became the official slogan in the early 1980s. Many Algerian factories were built close to Mediterranean waters in coastal cities of Algiers, Annaba, Arzew,

This field has been irrigated for growing crops.

Oran, and Skikda. But construction and industry did not expand fast enough to employ everyone needing a job. Consequently, many Algerians sought work in Europe. Travel back and forth each summer to visit families has become a part of Algeria's lifestyle.

AGRICULTURE

Agricultural development has been a fight against geography, climate, history, and politics. Thirty percent of the people farm. However, they contribute only 6 percent to Algeria's economic output. Until the late 1980s, that figure kept shrinking in the face of unprecedented population growth.

Algeria is the second-largest country in Africa. Yet, only 3 percent of the land is suitable for farming, one of the smallest percentages worldwide. A mere 13 percent of the land is pasture. Add severe droughts, locusts, and encroaching desert, and some reasons become clear why Algeria has trouble feeding its own people.

However, the biggest problem restraining agricultural progress has been government policy. Emphasis on industrialization first led to Algerian dependence upon imports for 75 percent of its food needs. The government claimed to have equal interest in agriculture. But inequalities in funding, resources, and salaries told the real story. The government absorbed the most fertile land and kept access to water sources for industry. Any attempts to modernize farming with tractors, fertilizer control, and metal plows were directed toward collective national farms. Industrial workers had bonuses, social programs, education, and recreation opportunities not yet available in rural areas. As a result, the youngest and brightest abandoned the countryside for the city, leaving farming to less productive aging peasants.

Over half the farms are small, privately owned plots. Farmers barely subsist on what they can produce. Even with the agrarian revolution and new emphasis on farming, the private farmer essentially struggles alone.

Some relief may come as a result of Benjedid's 1985-89 five-year development plan. "Toward a better life" became the new government motto. Benjedid allocated budgets for improving rural conditions, health-care clinics, and educating and training peasants, in addition to modernizing food production. He further distributed more land to private farmers and increased public projects to better all land. The government stepped up planting of trees to hold back the desert and built roads and dams. Demand for meat and dairy products moved the government to update stock-raising methods and organize large poultry farms.

Algeria's chief crops are grains, citrus fruits, grapes, olives,

A date palm full of fruit (left), and the grain market in Ghardaia (right)

dates, and vegetables, mainly tomatoes and potatoes. Wheat and barley are grown mostly on private farms by outdated methods, but they are an important part of Algeria's overall plan to grow more food. The government converted considerable vineyards to grain cultivation after decolonization, when demand for wine lessened. Nonetheless, better land on hillsides was reserved for growing fewer high-quality grapes. Algeria still exports most of its wine to France, despite objections from French wine growers.

TRADE

French settlers turned Algeria's trade system upside down. Arabs, displaced from land that sustained them, relied on common markets for necessities. Manufactured goods replaced articles produced by village craftspeople. Highways, railroads, and airports created different trade routes and market centers, easing

In spite of modern transportation, camel caravans are still widely used in the desert.

out camel caravans. A new trade system for manufactured and agricultural products became controlled by a separate and foreign population. Algeria existed to provide a better life for colons, the French army, and their parent country.

After the revolution, the government moved to fill trade gaps left by the French exodus. Modern and traditional commerce blended. Private traders were allowed to stay in business if they accepted government control. By the mid-1980s, family-run businesses dominated the retail trade. Larger firms left by the French came under the direction of worker self-management. The state organized retail outlet networks to distribute the goods in many cities.

Most rural Algerians still shop at *souks*, large fairlike markets where individual traders sell excess farm products or handicrafts from open stalls. There are daily, weekly, and seasonal souks scheduled in key regional centers as well as old sections of major

An open-air produce market in Biskra

cities. At harvesttime nomads from throughout North Africa come
to centers at Tlemcen and Ghardaia.

In early times, exchange was by barter: two traders swapped
goods to make a sale. Now usually money is used. After
independence, Algerian dinars replaced French francs for trade at
home and abroad.

Before the revolution, France imported 75 percent of Algeria's
total production. Declining relations with France during and after
the revolution forced Algeria to seek other foreign markets.
Algeria opened trade to all countries. Major trading partners in
the late 1980s were Western Europe, Japan, and the United States.
Since 1981, France has regained its role as principal trading
partner with Algeria.

Although oil and gas dominate, other important exports include
dates, tobacco, leather goods, vegetables, and phosphates. Algeria
imports almost as much as it exports and is under tight

Railroad yards (left) at Algiers harbor, and a Trans-Sahara Bus (right)

government control to protect local goods. Major imports are goods to produce products locally, foods, consumer goods, and equipment to run the economy.

Algeria stands firm in its goal for independence. However, the country receives loans and technical assistance to spur economic development from West and East European countries, China, Canada, Saudi Arabia, and the United Nations Development Program. Specialists from these countries offer guidance for education, military, industrial, and health-care programs. In addition, Algeria plays a big role in assisting other African countries whose people need money, food, and shelter through the Organization of African Unity.

TRANSPORTATION

Large investments in transportation were made in the early 1980s. Colons built a road network to serve their coastal

The Trans-Saharan Road

settlements and the military. But north-south routes were needed to unite the country and promote trade. Within eight years, Algeria constructed three major north-south roads and three east-west highways linking Morocco and Tunisia.

Roads into the desert were a problem to build and maintain because of blowing sand. That is why paving the Trans-Saharan Road, sometimes called the "Road of African Unity," was a particularly impressive project. This highway begins at El Golea and goes south through Tamanrasset to the border, before branching off to Niger and Mali. Its construction improved trade with central African countries and made it easier for farmers at oases along the way to market their goods.

All transportation systems are under government management and under constant expansion and renovation. The main railroad line follows the coast and connects major cities. It links with Moroccan and Tunisian systems at either border. Plans are under way to double the volume of tracks by the late 1990s. Major truck lines are forecasted to run across the High Plateaus and to connect the High Plateaus with southern oil towns.

Algeria has international airports in Algiers, Annaba, Constantine, Tebessa, Ghardaia, Tamanrasset, Oran, and Tlemcen. Foreign airlines serve Algiers, Constantine, and other larger cities. The national airlines, Air Algérie, flies jets daily between major cities and towns and to many foreign capitals.

Shipping has made the greatest advances. Between 1971 and 1981, the Algerian fleet went from nine to seventy vessels, carrying about 25 percent of Algeria's goods. The Algerian National Navigation Company has become a world-class shipping line with oil tankers, cargo ships, and passenger ferries. Seventy percent of the cargo passes through the main ports of Algiers, Annaba, and Oran.

COMMUNICATION

The field of communication continues to be a growth area for Algeria. In the mid-1970s, Algeria had one of the lowest ratios of telephones per population worldwide. Ten years later the goal was to have fifteen telephones for every one hundred citizens, in addition to linking Algeria to many other European countries.

Algeria became a world leader in launching earth-satellite communications for internal and international use. Now there are seventeen ground stations providing telephone, television, and telex services to the remotest areas of the country.

All media—radio, press, television, films, and book publishing—are owned by the government, directly or through the FLN. Government leaders view media as a way to reinforce Socialist and Arab nationalist goals. While Algeria claims freedom of the press, there is censorship of material too critical of the government.

Chapter 6

THE GUIDING FORCE
OF ISLAM

Islam has been more than a religion to Algerians. During the darkest colonial days, Islam provided a common culture that bound Arabs together. The more France tried to erase symbols of Algeria's past, the more Arabs clung to Islamic custom and thought. The strength Algerians gained from Islam became one of the main causes for Algerian nationalism.

Today, Algerians vary in how strictly they observe rituals of their faith. However, their view of everyday life and the world is a reflection of the teachings of Allah, their God. No aspect of modern Algeria—whether law, economy, dress, government, or social actions—is untouched by the traditional Islamic past.

ISLAM COMES TO ALGERIA

Islam goes back to the year 610 in the town of Mecca, a thriving trade center along a major caravan route between Yemen and Egypt. At this time a forty-year-old Arabian merchant named

An illustration of Muhammad with the Archangel Gabriel

Muhammad questioned worship of many idols. He also was bothered by inequalities between rich and poor in the name of religion.

Muhammad spoke of experiencing visions when alone in the desert. Archangel Gabriel told Muhammad that he was God's messenger on earth. As a prophet, Muhammad was to spread the word that there was only one all-powerful God—Allah.

Muhammad traveled widely along trade routes calling for converts to his God. However, he excused Jews and Christians, whom he called the original "Children of the Book." They could continue their religious life as long as they did not interfere with Islamic practice.

At home, Muhammad's preaching angered the people of Mecca. After a failed plot to kill him, Muhammad and his followers fled to Yathrib. Here people accepted his teachings. Yathrib became

The Ascension of Muhammad as depicted by an artist

known to Muslims as Medina, "the city." And Muhammad's escape, or *hijra*, in 622, marked the beginning of Islamic history and the first year of the Muslim calendar.

News of Muhammad's beliefs spread. Soon he was able to raise an army to fight the Meccans. In 630 his followers returned to Mecca, destroyed idols, and turned the pagan temple into a *mosque*, a Muslim house of worship. Finally, Meccans adopted Islam and accepted Muhammad as their spiritual leader. Mecca and Medina became Islamic sacred cities.

After Muhammad's death in 632, caliphs extended Islam beyond Arabia. Their driving armies launched successful holy wars throughout the Middle East and North Africa. Berber resistance in Algeria was great. Nevertheless, by the early eighth century, most Berbers adopted some version of Islam.

Through generations, Islam became divided into sects. The two

The Ain Salah Mosque in the Sahara

major divisions were Sunni and Shia. Sunni followed the Quran, the Islamic Bible, and traditions of Muhammad closely. Unlike the Shia or Shiites, they elected leaders from among the most worthy people.

Shiite leaders claimed loyalty through heredity. They honored Ali, Muhammad's son-in-law, as his successor. Shias accepted the Quran, but only some codes for living. Shia gained strength under the Fatimids, but lost importance after the first century of Islam. Today, very few Algerian Muslims follow Shia. Most are Sunni.

BASIC TEACHINGS OF ISLAM

Muhammad's followers preserved his words from God in a holy book called the Quran, meaning "recitation." Scholars wrote Muhammad's sayings and teachings as well as his personal code of behavior into the *hadith*, meaning "traditions." Together these writings guide moral, spiritual, and social life in most Muslim countries, including Algeria.

The Quran dictates that people are to be honest, patient, hard-working, and generous. Mistreatment and disrespect are condemned. Gambling and moneylending are prohibited, as are alcohol and eating pork. As in the Bible the Quran outlaws cheating, killing, and stealing. Punishment for these crimes gives back to the criminal what that person did to another. "An eye for an eye" follows the Old Testament law of justice with revenge.

Muslims are very proud of their faith and feel they are a chosen people. To Muslims, their God is the supreme being over all people and all time, even in the afterlife. Life on earth is a testing ground for life in Paradise after death. To gain entry into Paradise, rather than a hell of pain and suffering, Muslims are to do their best and be of service to others. Above all, they are to put their faith in God's will to be just.

FIVE PILLARS OF FAITH

To prove their faith in Islam, Muslims are to carry out "five pillars," or duties.

Basic Islamic belief holds that, "There is no God but Allah, and Muhammad is his Prophet." Certain ceremonies require repeating this statement, or *shahadah*. The *imam*, or prayer leader, answers the statement by declaring the speaker a Muslim.

Five times a day—at dawn, noon, midafternoon, evening, and nightfall—*muezzins* chant the call for prayer, or *salat*. In cities loudspeakers broadcast the time to faithful Muslims. Those who are too far away to hear determine the correct time by the sun. People can pray wherever they are—in the field or mosque—as long as they follow prayer rituals. On Friday, however, men have a duty to pray with an imam. Women may pray at a mosque in a

Left: People kneeling in prayer in a street in Algiers on a Friday midday, the Muslim's most important day of the week. Above: Mecca, the holy city of Islam

section separate from men. More often, women choose the privacy of their home for prayer.

Before prayer at the mosque, Muslims wash their hands, face, arms to the elbow, and feet. Once inside, the imam faces Mecca with rows of men behind him. Women, usually unwelcome at the mosque, stand behind the men. Everyone prays by reciting portions of the Quran. At certain times, they kneel with their foreheads on the floor.

Friday midday call is the main prayer of the week. The imam gives a short sermon and announces any important news. Friday is as important as the Christian Sunday or Jewish Saturday.

The ninth month of the Muslim calendar is Ramadan, the holiest time of the year. Ramadan celebrates when God revealed the principles of the Quran to Muhammad. From dawn to dusk, most Muslims fast, or *sawm*. They cannot eat, drink, or smoke. Only children, pregnant women, travelers, and those who are in battle or sick are relieved of these restrictions. Since the Muslim

An intricately decorated section of the Quran

calendar follows a lunar year, Ramadan comes in all four seasons over a thirty-year period. Ramadan is a great hardship in summer when steamy days last until eight at night.

In the early days when Islam began, there was a tax on personal property to be given to the mosque or the needy. Today, charity, or *zakat,* is a private concern of the believer.

The Quran charges all able Muslims to make at least one pilgrimage, or *hajj,* in their lifetime to Mecca for prayer during Ramadan. Several rituals and many days of prayer and trials mark the pilgrimage. Pilgrims begin by bathing outside the city. Men put on white seamless garments. Women wear black robes and veils.

One of the most important ceremonies of hajj includes encircling the shrine seven times and touching the blessed black stone embedded in the wall. The stone is the last trace of pilgrimages made by the prophet Abraham before Muhammad. Legend says the stone was originally white. But it turned black from the "sins of man."

The final or tenth day of hajj is for celebration throughout the Islamic world. At the final Feast of Sacrifice, worshipers slaughter goats, camels, or sheep and offer the meat to the poor. Muslims everywhere celebrate this day by gathering and exchanging gifts. When the pilgrimage ends, worshipers are honored by adding "al Hajj" before their name. Often, the journey climaxes a lifetime of working and saving.

SPECIAL DAYS

Beside daily prayers and Ramadan, Muslims celebrate many other Islamic holidays. *Ashura* signals the beginning of the Muslim year. It is the tenth day of the first month called Muharram. Ashura marks a day of mixed sorrow and happiness. There is a new year, but a passing of the old. Certain areas celebrate with joyous bonfires as most Muslims give alms and mourn their dead at cemeteries.

The twelfth day of the third month of Rabia al Awal is *Mulud*. On this day Muslims honor the birth of the prophet with lively festivities for children, some firecrackers, and plates of dried fruits.

After the trials of Ramadan, Muslims are happy to celebrate *Aid es Seghir* on the first day of the tenth month, Shawwal. Families prepare for "the little day, the little feast" by scrubbing their houses and painting the shutters. On the feast day, all dress in their holiday best and bring pastries to friends and relatives.

In addition to religious holidays, there are events occurring year around that call for families to rejoice together. Births, followed by formal baby namings, and circumcision for boys are all festive occasions.

Left: Veiled tribesmen at a Tuareg wedding
Right: Women from Tassili-n-Ajjer dancing at a tribal celebration

Weddings are celebrated with considerable pageantry and ritual, although customs vary from region to region. Devotion to details is important to the strength of the new family. Generally, marriage festivities extend for days. Extending celebrations allows time for the two families to bind together. The traditional bride experiences a ritual bath and days of song and sweets before being carried by her wedding attendants to her new husband. After the union, partying goes on for another week when the bride takes another ritual bath. The groom pays for the long party as part of the celebration of the marriage.

ISLAM IN ALGERIA

Algerians express Islam in many forms. Almost every Algerian is a Muslim. However, everyone does not follow Islamic rules faithfully. For example, only about 50 percent of the men pray at mosques each day. And rural Algerians follow diet and drink restrictions more strictly than those in urban areas.

Still, there is a strong feeling about being Islamic that overrides any location, laws, or beliefs. Algerians take pride in their religion. Even nonpracticing Arabs acknowledge the influence of the prophet. Repeatedly, people use phrases like, "If God wills it," or "In the name of God." Muslims believe everything is in God's hands. Religion is Algeria's lifeblood.

In earliest times, rural people practiced Islam laced with Berber spiritualism. *Marabouts*, or local holy men, guided the nomads with special mysterious powers from God. These remarkable blessings, or *baraka*, helped marabouts perform miracles and have unusual insights.

Followers of marabouts formed religious orders called brotherhoods. Brotherhoods had their own magical practices and ceremonies in addition to Islamic observances. Therefore, brotherhoods became increasingly isolated from educated Arab life. Traditional Islam viewed marabout teachings as counter to a united Algeria.

Brotherhoods reached their heights during the fifteenth and seventeenth centuries. Their popularity has declined since then. The French discredited marabouts as religious fakes. And postrevolutionary governments rejected any departure from centralized state religion. Nonetheless, isolated brotherhoods survive among the Kabyles despite greater government control over religion.

For most Algerians, Islam is a natural part of state reform. The government acts as religious adviser through the ministry of religious affairs, creating what some observers call "official Islam." Official Islam fits with the government's idea of modernization. The state monitors religious education, books, and Friday sermons. All mosques and imams are under government influence. Even the *sharia*, or Islamic law, blends with more modern laws handed down from the French.

Each government has acted to define Islam. Boumediene converted all Christian churches into mosques and demanded strict observance of Ramadan. He also reduced wine production and ordered the official Algerian weekend changed from Saturday and Sunday to Thursday and Friday. Devotion to Islam was to go hand in hand with modern technology.

By the late 1970s, younger Algerians became dissatisfied with the problems of living in an urban developing society. They looked to a purer, more fundamental Islam to give structure and meaning to society. Mosque attendance increased. So did requests for prayer rooms at universities and places of employment. Soon Islamic fundamentalist youths attacked more liberal university students and women without veils. "Wildcat" mosques sprang up to counter government-controlled worship. Muslim militants called for a new "Algerian Islamic Republic."

Benjedid's government suppressed violence and maintained control over religious affairs. But isolated outbursts got stronger and more frequent in the 1980s. Meanwhile, pure Islam experienced a revival throughout the Arab world during the 70s and 80s. A shaky economy with overcrowded cities of unemployed youth contributed to traditional Islam's rebirth in Algeria. The challenge for the future is to redirect traditional Islam toward keeping Algeria pointed in a modern direction.

Clockwise from above top: A young girl from
the Aurès Mountains area, a child carrying firewood
on his donkey, two men conversing in a market,
and a young woman from Ahaggar

Chapter 7
EVERYDAY LIFE
IN ALGERIA

DIVERSE PEOPLE

Through the years, Algeria has become a place where diverse cultures cross. Just looking at the people today suggests the racial variety recalling the country's long involved history. Nearly all Algerians are Muslims of Arab, Berber, or mixed Arab Berber descent — derived from the same ancient Berbers. However, their mixed physical features represent each conquest and considerable intermarriage. Algerians are fiercely proud of their Berber and Arab heritage. But neither white or brown skin nor red or black hair influence social status.

LANGUAGE

Language is the primary way Algerians tell ethnic communities apart. Before Arab invasions, all groups spoke some form of Berber. As Arabs transformed North Africa, only Berbers in the most remote areas retained their language. When France tried to erase Arab culture in Algeria, they made French the first language. Arabic and Berber survived in the homes as a form of protest.

A handwritten book—Arabic is read from right to left

Today, Arabic is the official national language. Speaking and writing Arabic identifies Algerians with Islam, Arab culture, and other Arab countries. A modern form of Arabic is used for radio, television, theater, and public speaking.

Still, reorienting society to Arabic has been a slow process. The four main Berber groups cling to their own dialects, and French persists as a necessity for some businesses and in technical and scientific fields. Newspapers and televison offer French as well as Arabic. Of three radio networks, each broadcasts in a different language—Arabic, French, and Kabyle Berber. French is being phased out as an important language. But it is still taught in Algerian schools as a second language because of its place in Algerian communication.

ETHNIC GROUPS

Arabs who speak Arabic make up 80 percent of Algeria's twenty-four million people. How they live depends upon where they call home throughout the country. Almost half of all Arabs

Berber portraits

live in cities. Urban dwellers tend to be better educated and more invested in the Algerian state than rural Arabs, who are more loyal to their group. Often, urban Arabs look down upon their seminomadic cousins who speak a different dialect.

Berbers represent about 20 percent of the population. Mostly these people live in rural areas. Four main Berber groups are noted by their dialect, cultural differences, and where they live.

Kabyles belong to the largest Berber group and are most resistant to national government intrusion. "Follow the path of your father and grandfather," is an old Kabyle saying followed to this day. Kabyles live in the Kabylie Mountains just east of Algiers. More recently, many Kabyles migrated to coastal cities or to France in search of jobs, but they tend to stay together in clans. In their mountain villages, Kabyles are governed by village councils of all the adult men. Their women are the most restricted of all Berbers, unable to inherit property or remarry without consent of their divorced husbands.

Chaouias have half the numbers as Kabyles. They have lived in the Aurès Mountains of eastern Algeria since the first wave of

Left: Men sitting at an outdoor café in the Aurès Mountains
Right: The city of Ghardaia, one of the seven cities in which the M'zabites live

Arab invasions. Through the centuries Chaouias isolated their groups, either by farming in the north or following herds in the south. Only Kabyle peddlers or desert camel herders visited Chaouia villages. During the revolution, the French herded many anti-French Chaouias into concentration camps, disturbing the seclusion that had lasted for centuries. Chaouia men believe their women have special magical powers. This belief gives women slightly more privileges than Kabyle women.

M'zabites live behind seven walled cities along the northern Sahara near Wadi M'zab, which lent its name to the group. The M'zabites, too, stay separate from the rest of the world. In fact, they call themselves "God's family." M'zabites follow a strict form of Islam and abide by their own religious government of elders. M'zabite Islam provides social equality and literacy for men and women. However, women are not allowed to leave the oases villages. Only M'zabite men can seek employment outside the village as merchants. By the mid-1980s, M'zabites built a retail trade that extended to Algiers. No matter where M'zabites live, however, they always return to the desert.

Among the Tuaregs, it is the men who veil their faces.

Tuaregs have been the most independent of the Berber groups. Their name comes from *tarek*, meaning "abandoned one," and it was given by frustrated Islamic preachers who found these nomads unwilling to practice Islam centuries ago. Their freewheeling desert culture, dominated by women rather than men, remained an oddity, even among Muslims. Legend states that a Berber princess from Morocco journeyed across the severe desert with only her slave girl as companion. For her courage she was made a leader—the first of a long line of female rulers. Tuareg women control the economy and property, and boys *and* girls study the Quran. Through the years Tuareg men, and not women as with other Muslims, wore veils. The custom proved practical as protection against sandstorms in the days men roamed the Sahara on camels leading salt, gold, and date caravans. As drought, technology, and the new government advanced upon the Tuaregs, nomads settled in desert oases such as Tamanrasset. Today, some Tuaregs even work on Saharan gas and oil fields.

At independence there were about 1 million foreigners in Algeria. As non-Muslims this group had French citizenship. Since non-Muslims felt more a part of European than Arab culture, they fled Algeria in droves. By the early 1980s there were only about 117,000 foreigners left in Algeria. They comprised small Jewish and Protestant communities and a slightly larger Catholic group. Of these, 75,000 were European, including 45,000 French.

POPULATION GROWTH

The average Algerian woman has between seven and nine children. At 3.2 percent growth each year, Algeria is one of the faster growing nations worldwide. In the twenty years following independence, Algeria doubled its population. If the current growth rate continues, Algeria will double its population again within another twenty years. Understandably, there is concern that having so many people endangers the country's economic growth. Already food, housing, and jobs are limited.

High birthrates, coupled with considerable loss of life during the fight for independence, created a young population. By the mid-1980s, more than half of Algeria's population was under age nineteen. Most of these youths never experienced the painful development of an independent Algerian society. Their experiences were with an overbearing government, unemployment, food shortages, and overcrowded housing.

THE FAMILY

For most people in the countryside and many in cities, the family is the most important part of life. Family loyalty overrides any personal relationships and responsibilities. Before the revolution, the basic Algerian family extended beyond a married

The members of a nomad family pose in front of their tent.

couple and their unmarried children. It included married sons and their families, grandparents, and widowed or divorced daughters and aunts and their children. Everyone took part in raising the children and everyone had a place to live. When the group grew too large, some families separated into another family unit. Since independence, there has been a trend toward smaller families and fewer children, especially in cities among the young and better educated. However, family ties are just as strong.

One area that remains the same is the family's traditional role in arranging marriages. Algerian men and women have little opportunity to mingle socially. So parents or hired professional matchmakers negotiate a marriage agreement. The ideas of romantic love so popular in Western movies, advertisements, and television have little bearing upon Algerian unions.

MEN AND WOMEN

Roles for men and women are well-defined in Algerian society. Women are generally viewed as weaker in all respects. Therefore,

Men, meeting in a market square (left) or at a coffeehouse (right), are the ones who socialize outside the home.

men have authority to make most major decisions involving money, property, and contact with outsiders.

The traditional women's role is to obey and serve men within the household. Young girls are taught that they are inferior to boys and their place is in the home. Boys, in turn, learn that women are there to comfort and take care of them. They, as men, will live in a world of mosques, marketplaces, and coffeehouses.

A veil covering all but the eyes serves to keep women in their place. Women are veiled and hidden behind courtyard walls to keep them pure. Their only outside contact is with other women. About 50 percent of women in larger cities wear veils outside the home. There was a growing trend since independence toward deveiling. However, the trend reversed slightly as more incidents of attacks on unveiled women by Islamic fanatics made news. In remote rural areas veils are less important. However, outsiders rarely see women at all.

Some women thought the war for independence would liberate

them also. They fought side by side with men and headed households when men were at war. But the society failed to accept women's equality as a cause. Emphasis on return to Islamic ideals with strong family roles prevented serious consideration of women in government and the economy.

Nonetheless, some women made great strides in education and jobs, mainly in urban areas.

The greatest battle over women's rights was fought over the family code. For years the government tried to advance the legal status of women. However, Islamic conservatives saw any changes as moves to Westernize Algerian family life. Benjedid put aside the first draft of the code in 1982 because of opposition from vocal women's groups. Two years later a more conservative version slipped into law without debate.

Although women gained rights to child custody and to their dowries, the code guaranteed man's superior role within the family in deciding whether women work outside the home and also deciding about divorce. Men could still have up to four wives as sanctioned by Quranic law, although few did. Women were considered permanent minors in the eyes of the law—either needing a father's or husband's consent for most activities.

Equality is far in the future for most Algerian women. Still, women have made some progress. Women can vote and run for office. And the number of female wage earners has increased considerably since independence. However, 7 percent is a low figure for the number of women employed outside the home. Most of these women are in traditional female jobs working for the government as secretaries, teachers, nurses, physicians, and technicians. As of 1985, only one woman had attained the rank of government minister.

A man in a burnous *(center), and women (left and right) wearing* haiks

DRESS

Algerian clothing is a blend of Western style and Islamic custom, particularly in cities. Traditional dress for women and girls involves draping a long piece of cloth over the entire body into a *haik.* Haiks go over the head to hide the lower part of the face and cover layers of clothes underneath. Many rural women also hang several charms around their neck to ward off the "evil eye" that brings bad luck. In cities younger women wear Western dress. As a compromise, some religious, yet modern, women wear a black or white veil over their lower face only.

Most men and boys in cities wear variations of Western clothing. They have shirts, jackets, and either Western-style or fuller pants. Businessmen wear suits and maybe a *fez,* the felt hat worn by North African Muslim men. In villages, men can be seen in a long hooded robe called a *burnous.* A burnous is made of linen for summer and wool for winter. It covers layers of shorter shirts worn underneath. Tuareg men wrap five yards of indigo blue material around the head into a turban that also goes over their robes and hides all but their eyes.

Education is free for all Algerian children, although not all children attend school. The quality of education has improved greatly since independence.

EDUCATION

A major goal at independence was to transform Algeria's largely French educational system into a vehicle for creating an "authentic national personality." The government invested large sums of money each year to provide free education to all Algerian children. Lawmakers redesigned the program to stress needs of an Arab developing nation, emphasizing Arabic and technical studies.

Twenty years after independence, Algeria fell short of its mark. Bulging population and severe teacher shortages placed unusual demands on the new system. In 1985, 71 percent of all secondary teachers were foreign. And many secondary and university-level teachers continued to teach in French.

Despite these problems, education has made great strides. Before independence, few Arab children attended school. Now 90 percent of city children and 67 percent of rural children go to school. Education for girls was almost unheard of before. Today girls account for 38 percent of the enrollment in secondary school.

Algerian law requires children between ages five and fifteen to

Many Algerian homes have private patios that cannot be seen from the street.

attend school. Thereafter, students follow a general, technical, or vocational secondary track. Difficult exams decide whether pupils qualify for university education, technical institutes, vocational training centers, or work.

Higher education has opened to more Algerians. Previously, the only university was established by the French in Algiers to serve French students. The Arab government added major universities in Oran, Constantine, Annaba, and other cities. In addition, the government sends thousands of students to universities in Western Europe, the United States, Eastern Europe, and the Soviet Union.

HOMES

Algerians, like other Arabs, value their privacy. So they surround their traditional homes and gardens with high walls. A

Left: Mud and brick houses are built on terraces in Djanet.
Right: A new housing development in Algiers

heavy door in a wall opens to a corridor that leads to a bright patio with a flower bed or fountain.

Everyday living rooms of the house encircle the patio. A receiving room for guests doubles as a dining room. Usually walls are whitewashed as is the outside stone or brick. Older homes have ornate mosaics and tiles on the upper part of the walls and ceilings. Lower walls are kept plain except for occasional family pictures. Family bedrooms and a kitchen complete the circle. If the family is wealthy, there may be a second patio with separate quarters for women and children.

Architects repeat this traditional pattern in the smallest spaces. High-rise buildings, Socialist villages, farmhouses, and tar-paper shantytowns on urban fringes all have the same general plan of rooms surrounding a central open area. Even in mud and brick oasis homes, women work within a sheltered courtyard.

Typical dark-colored tents woven by the nomads of the High Plateau

Only nomads and Kabylie Mountain villagers break tradition out of necessity. Nomads of the High Plateau and Sahara weave goats' hair, wool, and grass into dark-colored tents. In Kabylie, one-room homes on a mountaintop are built of clay and grass or piled stones. A low wall splits the room into one section for the family and another for animals.

RECREATION

Algerian social life revolves around visiting family. Relatives call on each other frequently to share sweet treats and lengthy conversation. Outsiders are rarely invited. But when they are, they are treated with great hospitality and generosity. "When you come to our house, it is we who are your guests for this is your home," is an old Berber saying.

Similar to other Mediterranean people, Algerians like to go to beaches. The Algerian middle class enjoys summer resorts along the coast. Here families swim, water-ski, play tennis, and fish at modern facilities. Most families vacation in August, which is the time Algerians return from work in Europe.

*Young boys hang out idly on a street in Algiers (left),
while the rural boy (above) dutifully tends his sheep.*

Soccer is the most popular national sport. People of all ages play
and watch soccer matches. Young boys can be seen kicking balls
outside city housing projects. In rural areas boys must tend their
sheep, rather than play.

Girls are less visible at play. They are expected to help their
mothers. Some jump rope and play a version of the Western string
game between two people.

As children get older, girls are seen less and boys take to city
streets. Young men, especially the unemployed, hang around
street corners and cafés looking for activity. Despite the size of
some cities, there is very little to do outside of home, school, and
work. As of 1988, there were only eleven movie theaters, two
swimming pools, and one discotheque for Algiers' nearly two
million people.

A family eats a meal of couscous (left)
Berber women grinding wheat (above)

FOOD AND DRINK

Traditional Algerian cooking delights the senses with special blends of seasonings to make foods unique. Coriander is the chief flavoring throughout the Maghrib. In Algeria, chefs include ginger, hot peppers, pimiento, cumin, mint, cinnamon, onions, garlic, cloves, and parsley as well.

Many of these ingredients are used to make the national dish, *couscous*. Couscous is steamed semolina wheat surrounded with lamb or chicken in a bed of cooked vegetables and covered with gravy. Often, onions, turnips, raisins, chick-peas, and red peppers are added. Couscous mixed with honey, cinnamon, and almonds makes a dessert that tastes similar to rice pudding.

Another favorite dish for large gatherings is *mechoui*. Lamb is roasted over an open-air spit at the beach or in the village or garden. Guests pluck bits of lamb from the roast to eat with bread, usually French bread.

Tuaregs preparing tea

For drinks Algerians enjoy black coffee or sweet mint tea.
Children can drink apricot juice or *syrop,* a sweet fruit drink. On
poorer oases, Berbers eat traditional flat cakes of mixed grains.
Their drink is made from crumbled goat cheese crushed with
dates and well water. A strong brew of syrupy tea follows the
meal.

CULTURAL REVIVAL

Great emphasis was placed on restoring Algeria's Arab and
national heritage after independence. Each government called for
a revival of art forms—music, painting, crafts—that disappeared
during the colonial period. They allocated funds to restore historic
monuments and archaeological sites and create libraries and
museums recounting Algerian national history. The government
opened handicraft centers throughout the country to pursue the
ancient artistry of making rugs, pottery, embroidery, jewelry, and

A market displays woven rugs (left), a specialty of Algeria.
Street musicians (right) in Biskra attract a crowd of villagers.

brass work. The national Institute of Music reintroduced
traditional music, dance, and folklore originating from ancient
Arabia and Moorish Spain.

Literature made the most immediate inroads in defining Arab
nationalism. Algerian writers of poetry, novels, and essays
described Algerian attachment to the land and ancient traditions.
Others such as Kateb Yacine, expressed Algerian nationalism in
plays, a new art form brought by the French. Younger writers,
including Rachid Boudjedra and Assia Djebar, rallied current
causes, such as women's role in society. Most of these writings
however, were published abroad in French and distributed in
Algeria. The Arabic literary renewal is only beginning.

The art form earning the greatest acclaim at home and
worldwide is film. Most Algerian films are produced by the

The rhita, *or reed flute, is popular throughout Algeria.*

National Film Company, ONAPROC. Algerians have won several international film festival awards for dramas and documentaries about colonialism, revolution, and controversial social topics. Mohamed Lakhdar Hamina, renowned film director, won the 1982 Cannes Film Festival award for his film, *Desert Wind*, about the difficult lives Algerian women confront in a traditional society.

Efforts to blend a sense of historic identity with Islam and modernization policies have created mixed messages for Algerians. They practice traditional Islam at home and in the mosque. They learn science and technology at school. The government as well as various ethnic groups send messages via the press, radio, and television. And many Algerians who travel abroad for work and study absorb Western ideas. Achieving a single national personality is proving more difficult than expected.

The Mediterannean
coast near the city
of Tenes (above);
the oasis at
Kerzaz (right) with
a typical desert
water well in the
foreground

Chapter 8

TOUR OF ALGERIA

Major differences from region to region and town to town captivate travelers to Algeria. Much of the fascination stems from its location as a meeting place for three significant cultures. There are European Mediterranean influences to the north, Arab religious forces from east and west, and black African cultures to the south. Another attraction is the country's physical and historic diversity. Algeria has ancient ruins, coastal beaches, caves, Stone Age paintings, mountain skiing, and beautiful desert oases—all within its borders.

Nevertheless, tourism has been an essentially untapped resource. Only a few tourist centers have drawn vacationers from countries other than France, Morocco, and Tunisia. In 1976, the government made a major investment in tourism to tell the world about its treasures. The goal was to expand the tourist industry fourfold between 1980 and 1990. The newly formed Algerian National Tourist and Hotel Company constructed modern hotels for conferences and vacationers. These efforts, coupled with plans already under way to advance national cultural heritage and to modernize the nation, insure that vacationers will soon clamor to see Algeria's varied cities and unique landscape.

The Museum of Fine Arts (left), and Botanical Gardens (right), in Algiers

ALGIERS

Algiers is Algeria's oldest, largest, and most historic city. Phoenicians settled here approximately three thousand years ago. For almost five hundred years Algiers was a colonial capital under Turkish and French rule before becoming the national capital after independence. Since that time a new city has grown up among many reminders of earlier days.

Algiers is one of the prettier cities of the world. It is built on a hillside with European-style buildings surrounding an old Muslim town that overlooks deep blue Mediterranean waters. Flowers and palm trees line the main road leading into the center of the city where a bas-relief memorial commemorates African culture. Nearby, there is construction of one of three planned subways in front of a Moorish-style post office. And history lives in the Prehistory and Ethnographic Museum that was once the Turkish Bardo Palace. Historic whitewashed buildings blend with classic Turkish and Islamic architecture amid modern high rises and businesses—truly a spectacular sight.

Opposite page: The Boulevard Mohamed Khemisti climbs one of the hills in the center of Algiers.

Algiers

The harbor of Algiers

The old Turkish harbor is Algeria's busiest port. Fishing boats, yachts, and the Algerian navy share space with vessels carrying oil, wine, fruit, and vegetable exports. Gleaming white buildings built at the turn of the century line the semicircular bay and lead to the business district behind. Here many Algerians work for the government, banks, and international trade organizations. Others work in food processing, metalworking, and cement and chemical processing companies.

The most colorful part of the city is the famous *casbah*. Casbah is the Arabic word for a Turkish fortress. During French rule, native Algerians were segregated into this section. The area became a hotbed of anti-French activity throughout the revolution. After independence, the government wanted to move residents to new housing and proclaim the casbah a historic district. Algerians protested until the idea died. Today, the old Muslim town comes alive. Large numbers of children play ball in front of overcrowded dilapidated homes. A maze of narrow streets leads to the colorful souk, with its crowded lanes and open stalls of crafts, fruits, vegetables, and freshly slaughtered sheep hung in rows.

Apartment buildings in the residental area of Algiers

Climbing to the top of the city's hills is the residential area with expensive villas and apartment buildings. Hotels and shopping centers overlook the eighty-thousand-seat stadium to the west of the city. Ornate mosques dot the skyline everywhere. Algiers is a perfect site for the National Festival of Popular Arts, a cultural and folk festival, each August.

ORAN

Between Algiers and the Moroccan border along the coast lies Oran. Oran is Algeria's second-largest city and the one most dominated by European influence. The city was first built as a breakwater by Arabs from Spain in 903, and it later became a prosperous port under the Almohads and under Spanish occupation from the sixteenth to eighteenth centuries. The French designed Oran as a major "second city," which until recently had more cathedrals than mosques. Visitors still see French street signs and the nineteenth-century architecture described in *The Plague* by the famous French-Algerian writer, Albert Camus.

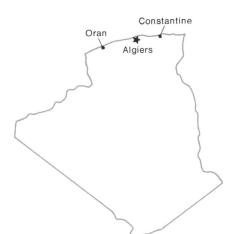

The city and harbor of Oran

The Opera House (left), and the fortress (right), of Oran

Much of Oran's charm parallels the sights of Algiers. Oran has a frontage road lined with palm trees along the Mediterranean. Elegant French houses mixed with modern office and apartment buildings overlook an imposing bay and busy harbor. There is Old Oran, too, with its Spanish cathedral and adjoining mosque. And up winding roads on a cliff overlooking the sea is the sixteenth-century Fort of Santa Cruz surrounded by Aleppo pine and carob trees.

The main difference is that Oran sits on high cliff plateaus that plunge into the Mediterranean. Beyond the city are the country's finest vineyards, power plants and oil refineries, and a series of beaches leading to Les Andalouses, the only resort village in the west. Here vacationers swim, fish underwater, and view wild swans off l'Ile Place.

Bridges connect the city of Constantine, which is divided by the Rhumel River.

CONSTANTINE

Constantine has one extraordinary quality—its location. Algeria's third-largest city and provincial capital is central to many of the most outstanding Roman ruins in the world. Located fifty miles (eighty kilometers) inland near the Tunisian border, Constantine stretches over the top of a huge chalk cliff. The Rhumel River dramatically divides the hilltop city, while several bridges connect the cliffside houses, university city, Old Town, Roman baths, casbah, Wilaya Administration, and business center.

Originally called Cirta under the powerful Numidian King Massinissa, Constantine was renamed by the Romans after Emperor Constantine. With Roman defeat, Constantine lost some of its splendor until the Turkish regency made the city its capital in the east.

The map shows Algiers and Desert regions.

The rocky terrain of the
Ahaggar (right) is a stark
contrast to the lush growth of date
palms crowded around an oasis.

Left: Watermelons for sale at El Oued oasis
Above: Traditional folk dance at an oasis festival

THE DESERT

The desert seems a highly unlikely place to travel, with limited tap water, extreme heat, gusting winds, and an abundance of crickets and scorpions. Yet, there are many surprises on oases throughout the wondrous desert. Picturesque villages provide a living history of Algerian life. Architecture varies with the breathtaking landscape. Walled cities and towns built into mountains hold low, earth-colored houses that change color with the landscape. Colorful apricot, pomegranate, and peach groves join date palms to attest to the fertility etched out of sand.

Most oasis towns have marketplaces with traditional handicrafts and, of course, mosques. Each spring there are folk festivals for dance and music, horseracing, and product festivals. Modern hotels offer air conditioning, swimming pools, shops, native dancing after dinner, and tours to ancient rock engravings and Berber ruins. But the biggest attraction to oases is Algeria's greatest natural resource, the desert.

The landscape near Djanet

ALGERIA—THE LAND

The same is true for all of Algeria. The *land* is what has drawn people to Algeria's borders for centuries. The land is Algeria

Earliest society depended upon the land. ''The land should belong to those who work it,'' was the basis of traditional Algerian political culture. Invaders tried to change that culture and the way the land was used. But invaders came and went. What remains are Algeria's contrasting beaches, mountains, springs, plateaus, and desert. Independence brought the land its new and rightful owners—native Algerians. Their inheritance nourishes and keeps them moving toward success as a major modern and Islamic country.

MAP KEY

Abadla	C4	Guerara	C5
Adrar	D4	Hardy	B5
Aflou	C5	Hassi Messaoud	C6
Ain Beida	B6	Hassi R'Mel	C5
Ain-Oussera	B5	Ighil Izane	B5
Ain Sefra	C4	Illizi	D6
Ain-Temouchent	B4	In Belbel	D5
Aissa, Djebel (mountain)	C4	In Guezzam	F6
Algiers (Alger)	B5	In Salah	D5
Annaba (Bone)	B6	Irharrhar, Oued (river)	E6, F6
Aoulef	D5	Kenadsa	C4
Arak	D5	Kerzaz	D4
Barika	B6	Khenchela	B6
Batna	B6	Ksar El Boukhari	B5
Bechar	C4	Laghouat	C5
Bejaia (Bougie)	B5	Le Kreider	C5
Beni Abbes	C4	Mascara	B5
Beni Ounif	C4	Mecheria	C4
Beni Saf	B4	Medea	B5
Benoud	C5	Melrhir, Chott (lake)	C6
Biskra	C6	Miliana	B5
Blida	B5	Mostaganem	B5
Bordj Amguid	D6	M'Sila	B5
Bordj Bou Arreridj	B5	Ohanet	D6
Bordj Viollette	D4	Oran (Ouahran)	B4
Boumerdas	B5	Ouallen	E5
Bou Saada	B5	Ouargla	C6
Charouine	D4	Ougarta	D4
Chelia, Djebel (mountain)	B6	Post Maurice Cortier	E5
Cheliff, Oued (river)	B5	Reggane	D5
Chenachane	D4	Saida	C5
Cherchell	B5	Saoura, Oued (river)	C4, D4
Collo	B6	Setif	B6
Constantine	B6	Sidi-bel-Abbes	B4
Dellys	B5	Sig	B4
Djafou	D5	Skikda (Philippeville)	B6
Djanet	E6	Tabelbala	D4
Djelfa	C5	Tahat (mountain)	E6
Djidjelli	B6	Tamanrasset	E6
Dzioua	C6	Tamanrasset, Oued (river)	E5, E6
El Alia	C6	Tazrouk	E6
El Asnam (Orleansville)	B5	Telertheba, Djebel (mountain)	E6
El Bayadh	C5	Tenes	B5
El Eulma	B6	Tiaret	B5
El Golea	C5	Tiguentourine	D6
El Meghaier	C6	Tilrhemt	C5
El Oued	C6	Timimoun	D5
Fort Lallemand	C6	Tin Amzi, Oued (river)	E5, E6, F5
Fort Mac Mahon	D5	Tindouf	D3
Frenda	B5	Tizi-Ouzou	B5
Ghardaia	C5	Tlemcen	C4
Ghazaouet	B4	Tolga	C6
Guelma	B6	Touggourt	C6
		Zaouia el Kahla	D6

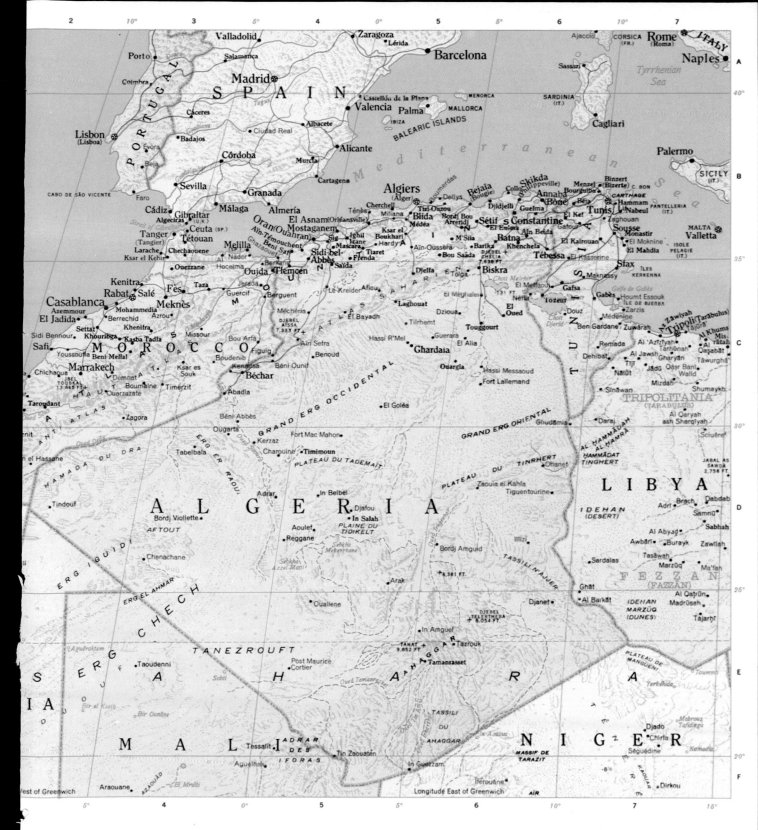

The center of the oasis at Salah

MINI-FACTS AT A GLANCE

GENERAL INFORMATION

Official Name: Al-Jumhuriyah al-jaz'iriyah ad Dimuqratiyah wa ash-Sha'biyah (Democratic and Popular Republic of Algeria)

Capital: Algiers

Official Language: Arabic. Berber dialects and French are spoken also.

Government: Under the constitution of 1963, the National Liberation Front (FLN) was the only legal political party. A strong presidential government with legislative power vested in a National Assembly was established. In 1976, however, a new national charter stressed Algeria's strong commitment to socialism. In 1989 a new constitution was approved.

The president, who is popularly elected, presides over a Council of Ministers and a High Security Council. Legislative power is vested in a popularly elected Assembly of 261 members.

Local government is based on the French model. The country is divided into communes, which in turn are grouped into diarates, and those are arranged into wilayas.

Religion: The country's official religion is Islam. The government pays for maintaining the mosques and training the mosque officials. Virtually all of the Algerian people are Muslim. Islam pervades all aspects of life. The problem of adapting and reconciling the teachings of Islam with the realities of late-twentieth-century life looms large.

Christianity came to North Africa in the Roman era. The Roman Catholic church was introduced after the French conquest, and the diocese of Algiers was established in 1838. Few conversions took place, however. There were several missions established, but they were largely concerned with charity and relief work.

The Jewish community is quite old and is also quite small.

Flag: The flag, officially adopted in 1962, has a red star and a red crescent against a background of green and white (left half, green; right half, white).

National Anthem: "Kassaman" ("We Pledge")

Money: The basic unit of currency is the dinar. In the summer of 1989 one dinar was worth $0.17 in United States currency.

Weights and Measures: Algeria uses the metric system.

Population: Estimated 1989 population—24,700,000; 55 percent rural, 45 percent urban

Principal Cities:
Algiers 1,721,607
Oran 663,504
Constantine 448,576
(Population based on 1983 official estimates.)

GEOGRAPHY

Highest Point: Mount Tahat, 9,578 ft. (2,918 m) above sea level

Lowest Point: Chott Meirhir, 102 ft. (31 m) below sea level

Rivers: Algeria's rivers tend to be seasonal or intermittent because of uneven distribution of precipitation. The basins of the Chelif and the Hamiz provide one-third of the country's irrigation needs.

Mountains: The Tell Atlas mountains extend up to 4,000 ft. (1,219 m) in altitude, while the Saharan Atlas mountains loom up to 7,000 ft. (2,134 m). Both mountain ranges descend toward the east and ultimately merge into the coastal plains of Tunisia.

Climate: Temperatures in the Tell, which stretches about 750 mi. (1,207 km) along the coast, average from 77° F. (25° C) in summer to 52° F. (11° C) in winter. The region receives little rain in summer but can receive 10 to 15 in. (25 to 38 cm) along the western coastline and up to 60 in. (152 cm) in the mountains.
In the Sahara desert temperatures may reach 120° F. (49° C). In summer, a hot, dusty wind called a sirocco blows northward.

Greatest Distances: East to west: 1,500 mi. (2,400 km)
North to south: 1,300 mi. (2,100 km)

Area: 919,595 sq. mi. (2,381,741 km²)

NATURE

Trees: Algeria has about 5.9 million acres (2.4 million hectares) of forests located in the Tell Atlas. There are dense forests of cork, oak, and cedar in the east and pine in the west. Deep green date palms grow on oases in the desert.

Plants: Plant life consists of tufts of several different kinds of grass, several stunted and sometimes spiny shrubs, and ethels, acacia, and jujube trees.

Animals: The climate is ill suited to extensive stock raising, but there are cattle, goats, and sheep. Few species of animal life are found—but there are some antelope, gazelles, hare, and a few wild boars, as well as a few birds and some reptiles and insects.

Fish: More than half of the Algerian fish catch consists of sardines. Pandoras, anchovies, whitings, and prawns also are prevalent.

EVERYDAY LIFE

Food: The Algerian diet consists mainly of foods made from grains such as barley and wheat. *Couscous,* the national dish, is steamed wheat served with meat, vegetables, and a souplike sauce. Algerians also enjoy Western-style cooking. *Mechoui* is a favorite dish at large gatherings.

Housing: Housing is one of Algeria's most pressing problems because of the high rate of population increase and the influx of people from rural to urban areas.

Holidays:

> January 1, New Year's Day
> May 1, Labor Day
> July 5, National Day
> November 1, Anniversary of the outbreak of the revolution

Culture: Since independence in 1962 the government has worked to strengthen the native culture that was largely repressed during the years of French rule. Culture draws increasingly now from Arabic, Berber, and Islamic roots. One of the most important art forms is literature. The literary art includes works written in French by Frenchmen living and working in Algeria: Albert Camus and Emmanuel Robles; literature by native Algerians such as Kateb Yacine also written in French; and poetry and plays written in Arabic or Berber dialects. Many contemporary works of literature are published abroad in French and distributed in Algeria.
Film is the art form earning the greatest acclaim at home and abroad.
The influence of Islam can be seen in many works of art—not only in the domed mosques that are found throughout the country but in rugs, jewelry, and handicrafts.
The country has many ethnographic and archaeological museums, a National School of Fine Arts, and fine examples of early architecture in its many old and beautifully domed mosques.

Sports and Recreation: Soccer is the most popular sport. Algerians enjoy both playing it and watching it. Going to the movies and going to beaches and summer resorts along the coast are popular recreational activities.

Communication: There are international airmail, telegraph, telex, and telephone services to the United States and Europe. The four daily newspapers and the radio and television stations as well are controlled by the government. About 16 percent of the people own a radio and 6 percent own a TV.

Transportation: Air Algérie, the domestic airline, serves Oran, Constantine, Annaba, and many of the Saharan cities, including Tamanrasset. Foreign airlines serve Algiers, Constantine, and other larger cities. There is railway passenger service between the major northern cities and bus service to many of the smaller cities and towns. Good paved roads, one of which links Algeria with Morocco and Tunisia, cover the northern region and connect some oases. Major construction projects of the 1980s included the Trans-Saharan Highway and roads to the Saharan oil fields and the construction of a tenth major seaport at Djen-Djen on the Mediterranean coast. The Trans-Saharan Highway is surfaced from Ghardaia to Tamanrasset.

All transportation systems are under government management.

Education: The literacy rate was only 30 percent in the late 1970s, and much of that competency was in French, not Arabic. During the late 1970s Algeria's educational system grew remarkably. Education now is free and compulsory to age 15. Despite government allocation of substantial resources, population pressures and a serious shortage of teachers have severely strained the system. The government has tried to accommodate to this by utilizing radio and television as teaching aids. By the 1980s the scarcity of qualified Arabic teachers was ameliorated by the importation of teachers from Egypt and Syria. In 1985 foreign teachers accounted for 71 percent of all secondary-level instructors. Algeria has begun to emphasize the establishment of technical institutes for training its people to work in the country's growing industrial economy. Each year Algeria sends some 7,000 university-level students to Western Europe, the United States, and also to Eastern Europe and the Soviet Union. But major universities now exist in Algiers and also in Oran, Constantine, Annaba, and other cities.

Health and Welfare: Algeria's free national medical program emphasizes preventive care. Newly qualified medical personnel are required by law to serve in state medical facilities for several years.

Algeria as a whole is covered by a network of state pharmaceutical agencies located in rural and peripheral areas.

The social-welfare system provides pensions for the old and disabled, allowances for families with children, and free health care for those under 16 and over 60. The country is still plagued by tuberculosis, venereal diseases, malaria, and trachoma.

ECONOMY AND INDUSTRY

Principal Products:
Agriculture: Wheat, barley, potatoes, citrus fruits, grapes, dates, olives, milk, meat, cork

Manufacturing: Liquid natural gas, refined petroleum products, iron and steel, transport vehicles, construction materials, textiles

Mining: Natural gas, petroleum, iron ore, phosphate rock, iron, gas, lead

IMPORTANT DATES

3000 B.C. — Berbers migrate to Algeria from southwestern Asia

1200 B.C. — Phoenicians found trading posts along North Africa coast

201 B.C. — King Massinissa battles Carthaginians at Zama, is given Numidia by Romans and opens northern Algeria to advances in agriculture, economy, and culture

146 B.C. — Romans destroy Carthage and move into Numidia

A.D. 100 — Romans banish Jews from what is now Europe to North Africa

313 — Emperor Constantine adopts Christianity, Christianity becomes official religion of Eastern Roman empire, including present-day Algeria

429 — Vandals conquer North Africa

534 — Byzantines drive Vandals from North Africa

632 — Death of Muhammad; Muslim armies spread Islam

911 — Fatimid Dynasty claims central Maghrib

1042-1147 — Almoravids govern the Maghrib and Spain

1147-1269 — Almohads instill a common culture in the Maghrib

Sixteenth to nineteenth centuries — Piracy becomes big business

1510 — Spain controls Algiers by occupying Penon Island in Bay of Algiers

1518 — Turks begin 300-year domination of Algeria

1815 — Barbary Wars, United States naval captain Stephen Decatur ends tribute taking by pirates

1830 — Piracy in North Africa ends; French capture Algiers

1834 — French declare North African coast a French colony

1840 — Abd al Qadir leads Arabs against French

1847 — Muslim Algerian holy war against the French ends; European emigration to Algeria begins

1871 — A serious anti-French rebellion by the Berbers occurs

1909—The University of Algiers is founded

1914—French occupy all of the Saharan region of Algeria

1914-18—Algerians fight in French army in World War I; 25,000 die

1926—First anti-Colonialism group is founded by Messali Hadj

1937—The anti-French Algerian People's party is formed

1939-45—Algerians fight with Allies in World War II

1942—70,000 British and American troops land at Algiers and Oran

1945-62—Algerians agitate for independence

1947—General Charles De Gaulle insists that Algeria remain a French colony

1954—Algerian War begins

1956—Large oil deposits are discovered in eastern Sahara

1958—Natural gas deposits are discovered

1959—De Gaulle offers Algeria a promise of independence

1960—De Gaulle calls on French army to restore order in Algeria

1961—FLN leaders meet with French government officials in France to try to bring about peace

1962—Algeria achieves independence; Ben Bella becomes premier; Algerian National Assembly is elected; Algeria becomes member of the Arab League and the United Nations

1965—Ben Bella ousted by coup; Boumediene takes command of the government

1968—Government begins to nationalize all foreign-owned companies

1971—Boumediene launches five-year plan for industrial independence; French oil and natural gas facilities are nationalized

1974—Foreign Minister Abdel Aziz Bouteflika elected president of United Nations General Assembly

1976—National charter adopted

1979—Benjedid elected president

1980s — Algeria negotiates disputes between Iran and Iraq, Syria and Jordan, and factions within Lebanon

1984 — Benjedid reelected

1985 — All French laws declared invalid

1988 — Benjedid elected to third term

IMPORTANT PEOPLE

Ferhat Abbas (1899-1985), leader for Algerian independence; formed Friends of the Manifesto and Liberty (AML); first president of provisional government of Algerian republic

Abd al Qadir (1807?-1883), hero, called "Sultan of the Arabs," Arab freedom fighter; finally surrendered to French (1847); his banner became national flag

Ali, (600?-661), cousin and, as husband of Fatima, son-in-law of Muhammad

Saint Augustine (354-430), author, bishop of Hippo; called for early separation of church and state

General Belisarius (c.505-565), Byzantine general; led expedition to drive Vandals out of Algeria in 6th century

Ahmed Ben Bella (1918-   ), underground leader; helped plan Algerian revolution; president; general secretary of FLN

Chadli Benjedid (1929-   ), colonel; third president, elected 1979, 1984, 1988

Houari Boumediene (1927-1978), ALN chief of staff; defense minister; president (1965-78); brought Algeria to leadership in the Arab world

General Thomas Bugeaud (1784-1849), French general who opposed Abd al Qadir's forces; governor of Algeria (1841-47)

Albert Camus (1913-60), French-Algerian novelist, journalist, playwright, and essayist

King Charles X, of France (1757-1836), dispatched troops to Algeria in 1830

Emperor Constantine I (?-d.337), Roman emperor, adopted Christianity as official religion of the Roman Empire (including North Africa)

Stephen Decatur (1779-1820), United States naval officer in the Barbary Wars (1815); protector of American ships against pirates

Viscount Exmouth (Edward Pellew) (1757-1833), British admiral (1816); fired on Algiers until Algerians agreed to end revenge against Christians

Fatima (c. 606-632), daughter of Muhammad; married Ali, cousin of Muhammad; from them the Fatimid Dynasty of northern Africa claimed descent

King Ferdinand, of Spain (1452-1516), called "the Catholic"; aided Columbus in his voyages of discovery

Father Charles Foucauld (1858-1916), French missionary; soldier in Algeria

Gaiseric (-477), Vandal, member of Germanic tribe; defeated Romans from Tangier eastward

General Charles de Gaulle (1890-1970), leader of the Free French movement; returned to France after liberation of Paris (1944); president of the Fifth Republic (1958-69); granted independence to 12 African territories

Dey Hussein (1773?-1838), last dey (representative of the Turkish sultan) of Algeria (1818-30); conflict with France occurred during his reign

Jugurtha (c. 160-104 B.C.), King Massinissa's grandson; one of the first fighters for Algerian nationalism; sought to reunite his grandfather's kingdom; led Berbers in revolt against Rome

Al Kahina, female chieftain; led first resistance in east Algeria

Khair al Din (Redbeard; Barbarossa) (1466?-1546), Barbary pirate; established Ottoman rule in North Africa

King Louis Philippe (1773-1850), declared Algeria a French colony in 1834

King Massinissa (238?-149B.C.), Numidian king

Ahmed Messali Hadj (Messali) (1898-1974), leader of Algerian workers in France (1937)

Micipsa (-118B.C.), king of Numidia; pursued policy of friendship with Rome

Francois Mitterrand (1916-   ), French interior minister at time of Algerian war; sent French troops to quell Algerian rebellion; president of France (1981-)

Mohammed el Hadj Mokrani, led Muslim farmers against French policies (1871)

Muhammad (c. 570-632), religious prophet; founder of Islam religion

Napoleon III (1808-73), emperor of the French; visited Algeria in 1860s

Raoul Salan, director of Secret Army Organization (OAS)

INDEX

Page numbers that appear in boldface type indicate illustrations

125

About the Author

Marlene Targ Brill is a free-lance Chicago-area writer, specializing in fiction and nonfiction books, articles, media, and other educational materials for children and adults. Among her credits are *John Adams* and *I Can Be a Lawyer* for Childrens Press; *Washington, D.C. Travel Guide*, a regular column for the secondary publication, *Career World*; and contributions to World Book Encyclopedia's *The President's World* and *Encyclopaedia Britannica*.

Ms. Brill holds a B.A. in special education from the University of Illinois and an M.A. in early childhood education from Roosevelt University. She currently writes for business, health care, and young people's publications and is active in Chicago Women in Publishing and Independent Writers of Chicago.

Ms. Brill has written *Libya* in the Enchantment of the World series. She would like to acknowledge the encouragement of her husband, Richard, and daughter, Alison—two people who particularly crave knowledge and appreciate a good book.